# TWiTCH
## and SHOuT

A TOURETTER'S TALE

# TWiTCH

# and SHOuT

## Lowell Handler

Foreword by Elkhonon Goldberg

With a New Afterword by Dr. Neal R. Swerdlow
of the Tourette Syndrome Association

University of Minnesota Press   Minneapolis • London

Published by the University of Minnesota Press
111 Third Avenue South, Suite 290
Minneapolis, MN 55401-2520
http://www.upress.umn.edu

ISBN 0-8166-4451-9

A Cataloging-in-Publication record for this book is available from the Library of Congress.

Printed in the United States of America on acid-free paper

The University of Minnesota is an equal-opportunity educator and employer.

12  11  10  09  08  07  06  05  04          10  9  8  7  6  5  4  3  2  1

For Lillian and Evan
"I am your brother Joseph."
GENESIS 45:4

*"Son, neurological disorder is the wave of the future."*
—My father upon learning of my diagnosis in 1980

*Here's to what the future brings,*
*I hope tomorrow you'll find better things*
*I know tomorrow you'll find better things.*

—Ray and Dave Davies, The Kinks

# Contents

*Foreword* xiii

Elkhonon Goldberg, Ph.D.

*Introduction* xxiii

Chapter 1.   Hitting the Road   1

Chapter 2.   Talk Isn't Cheap   16

Chapter 3.   Diagnosis   30

Chapter 4.   Drugs and Orphan Drugs   48

Chapter 5.   *Life* and Leukemia   64

Chapter 6.   Jet Set Tourette   88

Chapter 7.   Pot and Prozac Love   114

Chapter 8.   Susanna and Marriage   128

Chapter 9.   *Twitch and Shout*   142

Chapter 10.  A Second Chance at Life  162

Chapter 11.  Tourette Culture  176

Chapter 12.  Crazy and Proud  188

*Afterword*  205
Neal R. Swerdlow, M.D., Ph.D.

*Resources*  219

*Acknowledgments*  225

# Foreword

Elkhonon Goldberg, Ph.D.

I met Lowell Handler a few years ago through Oliver Sacks, a mutual friend, and am delighted to write an introduction to his unique and poignant book. While I knew about Lowell's Tourette, there was nothing in our occasional social interactions to betray the pain that accompanied his coming to grips with his condition and the inner strength that made it possible. The manuscript both impressed me with its evocative power and left me a bit shaken by pointing out how unaware we often are about the next fellow's anguish, despite the illusion of familiarity.

I am a neuropsychologist and cognitive neuroscientist. Clinical work with patients and research into the effects of various neurological conditions on the mind have comprised my daily activities for the last thirty years. Yet the glimpse into the inner emotional world of one affected by such a condition, afforded by Lowell Handler's book, is a powerful experience for me.

Our society traditionally treats a neurological disorder as a deficit, a loss. We see this in our terminology: aphasia—loss of language; amnesia—loss of memory. But if the norm is defined as average, then talent is, by definition, a departure from the norm. Hypermnesia and hyperverbality, infrequent as they are in our society, are regarded not as pathology, but as a gift. The relationship between talent and psychopathology has intrigued both clinicians and those afflicted (or blessed). Edgar Allan Poe wrote evocatively about the relationship between genius and madness.

Neurological and neuropsychological conditions may be marked by what we call "negative" and "positive" symptoms. Negative symptoms are those that reflect the loss of something we all take for granted, such as the ability to express ourselves verbally. Positive symptoms are those that reflect the emergence of some uncommon behavior or manifestation, such as hallucinations. Negative symptoms are intuitively comprehensible, easier to quantify and research formally. Positive symptoms are often more elusive and mysterious. They hint at a mind that is different and not merely deranged, a neurological condition whose abilities to both rob and endow are inseparably linked together. The link between genius and psychosis is evident in the lives of the artist van Gogh, the dancer Nijinsky, and the poet Rimbaud. Among the visionaries who shaped the history of our civilization, Alexander the Great, Julius Caesar, and possibly Akhenaton (the Egyptian pharaoh who founded the first monotheistic religion) suffered from epileptic seizures. Surges of creativity and productivity were interspersed with periods of extreme despair and mental paralysis in the lives of poets Byron and Tennyson, and the composer Schumann, who suffered from bipolar manic-depressive disorder. If talent often comes at a price, then, equally, certain neurological and psychiatric conditions sometimes bring their own rewards. These conditions remain the source of particular puzzlement and fascination.

Tourette's syndrome is one such condition, and particularly intriguing at that. What makes Tourette's so intriguing is that it is all positive symptoms and very few negative ones. First described by Gilles de la Tourette in 1885, this condition is variably characterized by uncontrollable facial and bodily tics, compulsive grunting vocalizations, profane verbalizations, and incessant exploration of the environment. These symptoms may appear in various combinations that change over time. They may vary from very subtle and

masked, to extremely conspicuous, when they are often perceived as asocial behavior.

A number of years ago, I salvaged from likely arrest a man
who was walking up and down the line of passengers waiting
to board a train at the Thirtieth Street Station in Philadel-
phia, compulsively barraging them with expletives. Reason-
ably convinced that this was a case of Tourette's, I interceded
with the police just as they were about to converge on the
man. On another occasion, I was taking a walk on Manhattan's Upper West Side in the company of Oliver Sacks, a
prominent student of Tourette's syndrome, and a friend of
Oliver's who had Tourette's. The young man's exploratory
behavior was extreme and was certainly drawing attention.
Everything on the street attracted him, a tree, an iron grid-
work, a trash bin. He examined the objects compulsively
and with all his senses. He looked, listened, touched. He
smelled them by bringing his face very close to the objects,
and tasted them by licking them with his tongue. When we
walked into a neighborhood restaurant, he immediately felt
up the middle-aged proprietress, who was, thankfully, a friend
and let it go. All this was accomplished in passing, interspersed
with a perfectly intelligent—in fact, rather intellectual and
animated—conversation on some high-brow subject.

The exact neurobiology of Tourette's syndrome is not fully

understood, but it is presumed to be closely linked to another puzzling condition, obsessive-compulsive syndrome. Attention deficit disorder and learning disabilities may also be associated with Tourette's. The symptoms of Tourette's are usually first seen in childhood and often abate by adulthood, but in some cases they persist through a life span. It seems to have a hereditary basis, but its clinical manifestations are often triggered by environmental stressors. Tourette's tends to afflict males more than females. Because of the diversity of manifestations, it is increasingly common to talk about the "Tourette's spectrum" rather than a single Tourette's.

Tourette's affects the neurotransmitter dopamine, one of the major biochemical systems in the brain, and neuro-anatomical structures called the basal ganglia, which are critical for the initiation of movement and more complex behaviors. Some scientists believe that in Tourette's the basal ganglia somehow elude the control normally exerted over them by the prefrontal cortex. The prefrontal cortex is probably the most uniquely "human" part of the brain, critical for intentional, goal-driven behavior, planning, and critical judgment. As we learn more about Tourette's, different subtypes begin to emerge, which may reflect different patterns of the aberrant interaction between the basal ganglia and the frontal lobes.

In addition to conspicuous behaviors, Tourette's often produces peculiar cognitive styles. Over the years, I learned to recognize a particular mental quirkiness, quickness, and jerkiness of thought processes. It may also result in a certain sense of humor, with wickedly unexpected turns of phrase or parables. This quick quirkiness of the mind parallels the quick quirkiness of the movements, as some Tourette's patients are unusually gifted at sports like karate and various ball games. When I try to conjure up the visual metaphor of the Tourettic cognition, Balinese dance comes to mind.

This book, which relates the curse and rewards of Tourette's syndrome, is the first such account written by a "Touretter." This is a quest of a man, forever set apart from the rest of the crowd by his rather striking peculiarities, to explain what it means to live with this strange disorder. "To those who have experienced it, no explanation is necessary. To those who haven't, no explanation will do," quotes the author. Yet his effort to "explain" is highly effective and the book is a richly satisfying narrative. It is also a poignant and courageous public statement, a call for dignity and understanding. In its candor, it is amazingly humane and unself-conscious.

This is the story of a young man tormented and puzzled by a mysterious condition that sets him apart from others.

We see him mocked and shunned yet determined to discover the source of his malady. We follow his path of self-discovery at various points of his journey from his diagnosis, which produces a complex mixture of relief, sense of inevitability, and the urge to run away from it, through his marriage and his relationship with his parents and siblings. In the midst of a family crisis, the usual roles of sickness and health are reversed, and as Lowell's tics and vocalizations become unbearable, he is no longer welcome even in their supportive circle. We see, too, the effects of his attempts at self-medication, the stabilization of his symptoms, and his ability to pull himself out of the morass of self-therapy gone bad through his work. Above all, we see an insightful and compassionate observer of human nature. Having been an "oddball" himself, Lowell Handler has a keen interest in the uniqueness and oddity of others. More than most people, he is drawn to humanity's weird, offbeat richness and grants it his acceptance and respect. He neither glamorizes nor patronizes. His sense of humor is playfully natural, not contrived. His narrative is as poignant and humorous as life itself.

Lowell's narrative is like nothing else I have ever read. If some narratives are "systematic" and others are "encyclopedic," then Handler's prose is "kaleidoscopic." It is a collage of episodes, impressions, and insights, one leading to another following an elusive internal rhythm. There is a disjointed spontaneity to it, both charming and poetic. Is the rhythm of Lowell's narrative a "photojournalistic" succession of frames, the result of his training? Or does it reflect the rhythm of his Tourette's?

Gradually, Lowell comes to grips with his condition and finds peace with himself and his Tourette's. It is a part of him for worse or for better. His Touretter friend Paige Vickery, a successful flutist and conductor, muses about a "magic pill" that might cure Tourette's. "What will it undo?" she asks. "It could take away part of who you are." Lowell seems to have reached a similar acceptance.

Lowell Handler is a multitalented man with Tourette's. His work as a photojournalist has brought him international acclaim, and now he is on the verge of establishing himself as an author. Has his talent developed despite his Tourette's? Is it coincidental with Tourette's? Or is it partly an expression of his Tourette's? These questions will never be answered definitively but must be on Lowell's mind.

"Neurological disorder is the wave of the future," Lowell's father once said, trying to console his son. In a way, Handler's father's crystal ball proved to be prescient. The popular naive dualism, which placed the diseases of the mind in a category entirely separate from the diseases of the body, is disappearing. One's mind is the function of one's brain, and one's brain is a part of one's body. The brain has been declared "the last frontier." The neurological conditions that were, until recently, ignored or regarded as a source of embarrassment and shame, such as Alzheimer's disease, autism, learning disabilities, and attention deficit disorder, are a greater focus of scientific research, as well as public interest and respect. Increasingly precise "cognotropic" drugs and more effective methods of cognitive rehabilitation are being designed by scientists. And voices such as Lowell Handler's are being heard by the general public, speaking of their conditions openly and proudly, calling for dignity and acceptance. One can live with Tourette's and enjoy a full and successful life. One can have self-respect and the respect of others. And one might even reap subtle benefits.

# Introduction

This book was written with the hope of better things to come, as the epigraph I've chosen suggests. In the twenty years since the events described in the first chapter, much has changed in all our lives. It is with this hope, and hindsight, that I look back on a journey that has taken me half my life, brought about much change, and showed me some far corners of the human experience.

From the mideighties until the midnineties, I worked primarily as a photographer. In 1990, I began teaching at the New School for Social Research, a university in New York City. At this time I also began to write about my experiences with Tourette and my travels with Dr. Oliver Sacks while researching and photographing a community of Touretters in northern Canada for *Life* magazine. The result of my early writing was published in the November 1991 issue of *In Health*, a magazine centered around issues in health and medicine. It was after I wrote and published this piece that the idea of a memoir began to take shape.

Nonetheless, the task in front of me was a difficult one. Along with Tourette, I have dyslexia and attention deficit disorder (ADD or ADHD), which often accompany Tourette and made my elementary school education difficult and frustrating. It wasn't until a year after I graduated from high school that I finished reading cover to cover my first book, the novel *Steppenwolf* by Hermann Hesse.

I don't think even I realized the isolation I experienced in a world without books, where letters inverted themselves or floated off the page, as if in a hallucination. I remember my childhood bedroom in my home in Bellerose, Queens, where my mother acquiesced to my acting out by playing a game with me that we repeated weekly. She said I could completely demolish the room if I agreed to help her clean it up when I was finished. I see now that this violent means of venting and releasing an overflow of energy was the direct result of my inability to express myself. Later, in high school, I resorted to smashing walls and breaking objects. My inability to understand my condition exploded in these unsubtle and inarticulate ways.

Making

pictures became my salvation. In the early
nineties, I returned to college and finished a master's program in media studies at The New School, where I became
more interested in photography and moviemaking, which
is how I have made my living. This way of viewing the
world has influenced everything I do, including my work
on the 1995 documentary *Twitch and Shout*. As a photojournalist, I am used to telling a story in pictures and as I
turned to my memoir, I was forced to re-create this method
of storytelling with language. The incidents in *Twitch and
Shout* may not follow a strict chronology. Instead, some
events of my life are highlighted or spotlit through the

prism of Tourette. Consider this memoir a series of frozen photographic frames, given as much movement and depth with words as I have been able to summon.

*Twitch and Shout* was written over a two-year period, but it was taking shape for decades. If others have written about Tourette syndrome in recent years, notably absent has been a full-length memoir by an individual with the disorder. This was one of the factors that encouraged me to write a personal account. In addition, I wanted to confess, explain, and articulate my thoughts in a way that would bring many other voices besides my own into perspective. Many of the people quoted in this book have Tourette, some do not. (Those people identified only by a first name have been given pseudonyms.) It is these individuals, whose voices call out from the pages, who helped me find my voice.

The time before this book begins represents the early days of searching and coping with undiagnosed Tourette symptoms and its effects on my family: my sister, Lillian; brother, Evan; and our parents, Murry and Enid. In the public high school I attended, Tourette syndrome was unknown. In some respects I am thankful for this, because it enabled me—even forced me—to experience a normal, mainstream education. Much credit for this goes to my parents, who treated me as they did my sister and brother, with care, direction, and love.

Now I look back on my life and see Tourette as an enigmatic tapestry, woven of patterns that seem unconnected and make no sense at all. But I also realize there is an order to it, a dance of symptomatology. Tourette is a rhythm of energy, movement, sound, discovery, touch, smell, taste, feel, and sight. It is a rhythm I am stuck with, which will continue for my lifetime and for the lifetime of everyone it affects. It is the electric and chemical rhythm of my cells, a living entity within an individual. Tourette is unpredictable yet has structure, and is faithful in the sense that it is always present. In other words, Tourette is part of life, not always good, but as I would come to see, an integral facet of an ever-evolving personality.

New York City

# 1. Hitting the Road

*C*rying and gurgling in my crib, I let out unbabylike
sounds: shouts, grunts, and hiccuplike noises. I remember my head, arms, and legs twitching rapidly. Any movement
nearby was a jolt to my nervous system, and as the shadowy,
blurry figures I would become familiar with passed by, I struggled to find a position in which to rest. I could not control my
body, especially my limbs. Each time someone came to play
with me, I flinched, blinked, and recoiled from these atten-
tions, feeling afraid. My parents wondered if this was custom-
ary for a fidgety newborn. Lowell will grow out of it, they
thought.

■ ■ ■

Sitting in my fifth-grade classroom, I attempted to suppress
the sounds that would later evolve into barks and hoots. My

head bobbed up and down and from side to side, with a rapid and purposeless jerking. The kids in class made fun of me, mimicking my noises and tics. Copying work from the blackboard was difficult, and I usually transcribed the text in mirror image, writing the inverted letters in my notebook. Unable to read, I was strangely at odds with the written language, while my movements made it difficult for me to sit still. Surely, my teachers thought, my "learning disability" could be corrected if I applied myself.

■ ■ ■

During my first year in high school, I'd walk down a crowded corridor feeling the need to jump in the air and kick the back of my thighs. This irresistible urge tormented me for months and finally, in full view of other students, I succumbed to the inevitable acrobatics. I also began to feel compelled to complete certain actions, touching things repeatedly or invoking a particular phrase over and over. My actions were embarrassing and my classmates harassed me. I couldn't explain my behavior, but I thought I was just nervous in my new surroundings. I would "settle down" once I adjusted to high school. I would learn to fit in.

■ ■ ■

There has always been trouble, but now it's getting worse. I am twenty-one years old. The jerky movements are not as bad as they used to be, but there are even more problems with my speech. Some words seem to become stuck in my throat and don't make it out of my mouth. Other words I feel the need to shout out, emphasizing individual syllables. Sometimes, though, I thrust my arm away from my body, almost as though I am shaking something. I keep thinking maybe there is something really wrong with me—mentally. Am I fooling myself by imagining all these disruptions will disappear in time?

I have dropped out after my second year at School of Visual Arts in New York City. I felt trapped in school, nervous with all of my twitching, head bobbing, and stuttering. I was fortunate to enjoy an atmosphere of great tolerance—nothing seemed to astonish these worldly students or their teachers—but I needed to know how I would be accepted (or rejected) in the real world, outside the college walls.

After leaving school I commuted from upper Westchester into New York City for six months to that fucking job as an audiovisual assistant at a large corporation, mostly preparing the slides for projection shows. The scripts were all coded to the slides numerically, and if you were off just one you'd blown it. It's true I did mix things up. I would often lose my place in the script or put a slide in the projector upside down or reversed. My boss Doris didn't know when she hired me that in addition to my various tics and twitches I had dyslexia, a neurological problem marked by a misfiring of chemical signals between the brain and the eyes or ears. There was nothing wrong with my sight or my hearing, but there was some glitch in the mechanism that carried information between these sites and the area in the brain where the information is processed. I couldn't read fluently until my late teens, and I still got visual symbols confused and reversed. After a few mistakes, my supervisor Steve brought me to Doris's office.

"What's going on?" she greeted me. "Sit down and talk to me." Doris was the wife of Tom Jay, a staff photographer at *Life* magazine for almost thirty years. I had been studying with him at his home workshop in Croton and working as his assistant. He had recommended me for this job. Now his wife was about to fire me and I knew it. Maybe I couldn't blame her, but I was seething nonetheless. Doris reviewed my evaluations with Steve as if I wasn't there, and then looked up at me and asked if I had any learning disabilities. I felt I had to admit I had dyslexia and sure enough she fired me. "I know about these things," she offered. "You know our daughter has some problems." I used to see the Jays' young daughter when I worked in Tom's darkroom. There was something strange about the girl, a little off in some way, but difficult to specify. At the time, I wonder if on some level I knew I had something in common with her.

I will fight it, I thought to myself as I cleared out my office. No, better yet, I will leave New York altogether and I will drive from one end of the country to the other and photograph everything I see. That's what I want to do right now—photograph and see.

∎ ∎ ∎

As the winter turns to spring, the only thing I can think about is hitting the road. This part of New York, the Hudson River Valley just north of the city, is beautiful, but I know I won't be here to see summer arrive. I wonder what I am running from. I wish I knew how to erase my strange speech and mannerisms. My mother and father can't help me and don't know what is wrong. Dad is strong, almost stern, but has always been supportive. Mom is gentle and understanding, but they have both been perplexed by my worsening problems. When I was a child, doctors said, "He'll grow out of it." For years my parents went with me to psychologists, psychiatrists, ophthalmologists, and optometrists. All this effort, expense, and searching ended with frustration, usually with the suggestion of "poor family dynamics."

On April Fool's Day 1978 I am ready, a little sad, feeling especially alone. I love my parents very much and will miss them, as well as my sister, Lillian, and brother, Evan. Lillian, who is between Evan's age and mine, has always been so loving and jovial in temperament. Evan, the baby of the family, just turned sixteen and has been imitating my friends and me—five years older than he—for the past year by growing his hair longer and listening to The Band. He has a keen interest in acting and will become caretaker of my rock-and-roll record collection. In the past year we've become quite close.

Dad has given me a '63 Saab he had bought years ago, which I pack with everything I own: clothes, camera equipment, sleeping bag, and a one-man tent. He said years later that after many teenage calamities he was glad to see me go. "I wanted to pack you lunch." But in spite of my father's black humor, we both know that I am leaving the only home I have known, and that I will not be back for a long time. I say my good-byes with a lump in my throat. Our next-door neighbor comes down and shakes my hand with a twenty-dollar bill tucked under one of his fingers. I thank him, get in the car, and drive away.

My brother, Evan, left, my sister, Lillian, and me in a simpler time, before my symptoms had a name. Photo by Murry Handler

I have no clear destination. All sorts of things go through my mind as I head south. Where will I go and what kind of people will I meet? What will I do when I run out of money? Most of all I wonder if I will be accepted. I am now stuttering often, my head jerking forward and backward. My leg twitches, sometimes with so much force I stomp my foot on the floor with a loud thump. I am edgy. Is impulsivity and spontaneity part of my odd condition, or am I just hyperactive? There is always some explanation offered by strangers to my "restlessness." "Are you cold?" someone will ask on a ninety-degree afternoon. Once an old woman at an inter-section eyed me and said, "Oh, so you want to dance!" Is this twitchy, erratic feeling characteristic of some under-lying disturbance unique to me alone, or simply the com-mon exuberance of an energetic young man?

I stop for the night, somewhere in Virginia, near the North Carolina border. As usual, I have to pick just the right spot to find relief from my tensions. It cannot be too close to the other campers, or too far. It also must be fairly flat, and without many rocks. The first spot I come upon is good, but too close to the others. The second has enough space, but too much dirt and not enough grass. Finally, I find the perfect spot. I feel settled for the night.

The next morning I pass Fancy Gap, Virginia, and cross Highway 77. As I come into Asheville, North Carolina, there is a sign reminding me that this is Thomas Wolfe's boyhood home. I think of his book *Look Homeward, Angel*, which I know from high school, and am momentarily homesick. The town seems a little run-down. I book a room at a simple motel for ten dollars and bring my few things inside. Later I drive around looking for a bar and find one full of college students.

I proceed to the bar and order a scotch on the rocks, my

drink of choice that year. I find the alcohol suppresses my odd movements.

"You are in the wrong state," the bartender says.

"What?" I respond, thinking, Here comes trouble.

"We only serve beer and wine, no hard liquor." Apparently that is the law. I have a beer and make my way through the crowd to a spot at the other end of the bar. I try very hard to inhibit my movements, particularly the leg stomping. The crowd is about my age—in their early twenties. I can't detect much outward difference between these students and me, except that I have quit school to wander around the country. Do these people have ideas and values that are somehow distinctly different from mine? I am reminded that appearances really tell us very little about ourselves.

Most of the customers look happy. Even I begin to feel at home. A noisy bar is the best camouflage for me. No one can hear the sounds I make and few people look at my strange movements, but even here I am not fully protected. Most noticeable are the jerking movements of my head, up and down and from side to side as I talk. What bothers me most, though, is the way I speak, shouting some words, others just squeezing out of my throat. I'd love to walk up to someone and say calmly, gracefully, "My name is Lowell. I'm from New York."

I stay at the bar for a couple of beers but realize I am not going to have any great social interaction here. I return to my motel, where I watch television and drift off to sleep. I feel that if I avoid human contact there will be less chance of an embarrassing situation or rejection. Alone, and in the quiet of my room, I am safe.

■ ■ ■

From Asheville I go through a couple of neighboring towns until I get to Route 441, one lane in each direction that goes all the way to Athens, Georgia. Beyond Athens is a smaller road that takes me to Macon, where I turn onto the superhighway that continues to Tampa, Florida. I have friends from high school there, and some companionship will be comforting. I am eager to get to Florida by nighttime, and as I drive toward the snarl of highway that approaches Tampa, I realize this is the first major metropolitan area I have been to since leaving New York.

It has been a year since I've seen Bill Morse and Joy Englander and in that time my strange manifestations have worsened. I try not to worry; after all, they are friends. We all greet one another as I walk into Joy's living room. "Lowell," Joy says as I kiss her, and put my arms around her and

Bill. Joy lives there with a roommate and Bill is staying in the living room until he finds a place of his own. I am going to stay with Joy's brother Stanton, who has a spare bedroom in his apartment. We sit and talk until it gets late. Stan is a very likable guy, easygoing and friendly, and we have our mutual interest in photography. But as the evening wears on Stan's roommate, Bob, keeps asking, "Is this guy for real?" He cannot believe my stammering and stuttering, my jerky movements. Bob thinks I am kidding him. To some extent, we all ignore my behavior because it is embarrassing not only to me but to everyone. Stan accepts me instantly due to familiarity, while Bob is bewildered, even annoyed, at my spasticlike movements.

On Saturday morning, Stan suggests the three of us visit Ybor City, a Cuban section just a few minutes out of town. We drive there with cameras, film, and flash. The club Stan takes us to is a huge bar and stage, with a number of smoke-filled rooms and pool tables where transvestites put on outlandish performances. Stan says he will handle all the arrangements for the pictures. I have seen him talk people into doing anything. We speak with the manager of the place, and he talks to some of the "girls" who are making themselves up. After a couple of beers they decide to let us go into the dressing room and photograph.

The "girls" love the attention. In the dressing room we meet Randy, a fairly attractive girl, for a guy. Stan talks to her as she looks into a mirror surrounded by lightbulbs. "You know you're beautiful," Stan says to Randy, and then he starts to take some pictures of her. The more Stan photographs and tells her how wonderful she looks, how sexy she is, the more responsive she becomes. Randy is mouthing kisses at the camera. She takes down the strap from her shoulder, and runs her hands through her hair. This is really wild, I think, and Stan suggests we continue photographing outside the stage door.

There is an alley out the door, illuminated by a single lantern. Randy leans her back against the brick of the building, and slides up and down the rough surface. She takes down the other strap of her dress, and actually begins to look very sexy. Her whole neck and a lot of her chest are exposed, and she begins to hike up her dress slowly. All this time, Stan is pouring it on: "You're flawless," he says, "beautiful." Randy slowly slides her dress up, and has no underwear on, but has no cock either—just a mass of black hair. Randy is now writhing in the dirt of the alley, while Stan stands over her and photographs. I don't even take pictures. It is great watching Stan work and I don't think I should intrude or compete.

In this moment I find something seductive about using the camera to obtain access to the subterranean. I want to explore the underbelly of life on my journey, photograph the seldom-seen outsiders of society. On some level, possibly even unconsciously, I want to force people to observe that which is usually ignored. If people are going to look away from me in shame because of my oddity, I will force them to see, through my photographs, every aspect of life, however vile or beautiful. And if people are going to stare at me and be unaccommodating, I will view them through the lens of a camera. I will watch those who are watching me and comment in a way on my own behavior. Those who watch will also be observed.

■ ■ ■

I stay in Tampa for a few days but get the feeling that I should look for somewhere to go for a while and stop this aimless wandering. I consider my options: I will either go to New Orleans, continuing my journey, or work on one of the shrimp boats that dock along the west coast of Florida. I find out that the boats come ashore at Fort Myers Beach, a couple of hours south of Tampa. I decide to take a drive down there and meet up with some of the boats that fish the gulf.

The drive along the shoreline is pristine, and my mind

drifts to Evan and the rest of my family. When will I see them again, and what will I be like a year from now? Will my condition be different? Will I be cured? Will I be worse? There are rows of palms along the road, islands in the middle of the roadway separating each one-way lane. The temperature is a perfect eighty degrees and it's been sunny every day. I find a section of beach with a dock built onto the sandy dirt and a couple of shrimp boats. I park my Saab and look for a fisherman.

"Hello," I say and tell him I may want work on one of the boats.

"We go out for two weeks, then come in for a couple of days, go back out again. You interested?" he asks.

"Yeah," I respond. "How is it?"

"It's OK. It gets old sometimes, especially when you have to work all night with the nets." I talk to him for a while and don't know what to do. I could use the money from fishing, but it seems like very hard work. I worry that I'll be trapped on this ship with my own strange movements for weeks at a time. Will a fight break out because of me? What do angry shrimpers do with twitching, stuttering New Yorkers if they mess up?

■ ■ ■

It's not only the noises now; my whole body contorts with a jerky swivel, especially my head. These constant movements are perplexing and disturbing. I wish I could start my life over again. I wouldn't be as nervous as this, like a time bomb waiting to explode. Through my travels, I am determined to find some peace of mind, a degree of contentment. All I can do is move onward. I will take it one step at a time. Tomorrow I'll head for New Orleans, the French Quarter, and see where I fit in.

# 2. Talk Isn't Cheap

**I knew it at first sight.** The French Quarter, New Orleans, with its incredible architecture, its seductive mix of charm and decadence, was an invitation to explore not just a city but myself. The Big Easy, it's called, and I was immediately at ease. Meandering through the old narrow streets I smelled Creole sauces, gumbo, beer, and honeysuckle. I heard sounds of distant rhythms from brass instruments, partying, and raucous conversation. The air was thick and sultry, with scent and sound wrapping around me like a humid blanket.

I had never seen anyplace like the French Quarter. The buildings are Spanish and French, erected hundreds of years ago with iron gates, balconies, and gardens. Brightly painted shutters on pastel-colored houses were poles apart from the gray and beige hues of New York City. All of the historic and fanciful architecture is densely packed into approximately sixteen square blocks. Juxtapose this with the sight of modern-day tourists, transvestites, and black and white visitors crowding the streets, often drunk from libation in "go cups," which apparently was legal. I turned the corner to Jackson Square and spotted a fire-eating juggler dressed in a colorful jesterlike jumpsuit. The crowd applauded with hoots and whistles, leaving coins in a cloth the performer spread at his feet. Behind the juggler was a large backpack. He was a vagabond like me, but with a better show to offer.

I wanted to stay here and photograph, shoot rolls of the scenes I was translating into black and white. If it was in my mind's eye, why not in my lens? I made an instant decision to stay on in New Orleans, so acute was the call of my camera.

The visual stimulation was exciting, but I had no idea where to sleep and only a few hundred dollars left. At sunset, I came upon a sign: Heads Inn for Weary Travelers. Inside a man informed me that for three dollars a night I could sleep on the balcony shoulder to shoulder with other boarders. We had to be gone by 7:30 A.M., because the building was used for other purposes during the day. I brought in my sleeping bag and a few belongings from the car and began a bizarre evening at the Heads Inn.

"Hey, where you at?" a man with no legs asked me. "How ya doing, my name's Nick."

Nick had long, light brown hair and was friendly. His body, with its muscular arms, ended at the waist and rested on a skateboard that he used for mobility. Nick's hands were caked with black dirt as a result of his method of propulsion.

"Hey, I'm Lowell," I shouted out in a stuttering fashion, the uneven jerky tone that characterized my speech. "Just staying for the night." Nick was talking to Bob, who was tall, at least compared to Nick. Bob had thick, wavy, jet black hair and was drunk, his slurred speech coming fast. Both men and a woman were eating from a large black garbage bag that had been collected from the street. Oblivious to the fact that they were eating other people's garbage, Nick explained he was a cook while he licked two dirty fingers full of what seemed to be tomato sauce.

"Linda," the woman said, extending her hand. "I stay here sometimes." Bob continued rambling about God knows what and seemed annoyed each time I opened my mouth to speak.

"I live here," Nick said. "You want to see my room,

Lowell?" The rooms at the inn were for weekly rental, the balcony being for one-nighters only. The rooms had clothes as well as belongings strewn about and were simple square boxes with no windows or bath. Once inside Nick lit up a joint and began to pass it around to Linda, Bob, and me. When the marijuana reached me I took long, deep hits and felt at least some relief from my tensions as I became stoned, while Bob complained to Nick about me.

"Do you hear the way this guy talks? I mean I don't care, but . . ." Linda was quiet.

"If you really didn't care," Nick said, "you wouldn't say anything. So what if he stutters." At that moment, I knew Nick and I would become fast friends. I wasn't aware of it at the time, but years later I realized I often form immediate bonds with others suffering one disability or another. Perhaps people with something wrong in their minds or bodies are bound together as with ethnicity, race, gender, age, or profession. This place was obviously an inn for outcasts, but I could qualify as an outcast even among outcasts.

People were beginning to stream in from the street for the night, and I wanted to secure a spot on the balcony. "Accommodations" were on a first-come-first-served basis. My sleeping bag and cameras were rolled up together along with some bathroom items and clothes. I laid out the sleeping bag and planned to spend the night with my cameras tucked into the bag to guard against theft. As the others got ready for sleep I realized Bob had ended up next to me, now extremely drunk, yelling occasionally. A toothpick-thin man to my right was wearing what

On Bourbon Street one night, I snapped a picture of this man dwarfed by signs and souvenirs of what the French Quarter had to offer.

looked to be sheets. He carried a huge cloth pouch, tied at the top, full of soybeans. I fell asleep to the sounds of his incoherent chants between chewing beans. At one point during the night Bob sat straight up and screamed at the top of his lungs. I turned to the soybean eater and saw he was still chanting. I took some comfort that it would soon be dawn, and I'd be gone.

■ ■ ■

I knew I needed to work and in my walks throughout the Quarter I had come upon a sign advertising for a waiter in a restaurant called Trios on Royal Street. I told Tony Marino, the owner, "I'm honest and I'll work hard."

Tony did not interview me for very long. "Our dishwasher didn't show up today. Would you be willing to work washing dishes tonight, and we'll start training you for waiting tables tomorrow?"

I didn't really want the job of dishwasher, even for a night. "Sure," I said.

I worked until midnight washing a huge pile of the night's pots and pans. Exhausted and not having a place to stay I walked directly across the street to the Andrew Jackson Hotel and paid twenty dollars for the night—exactly the amount earned from the dish washing.

Two other men worked at Tony's place. Daryl Evans was a black native New Orleanian who seemed quiet but was actually a wild young prankster. He worked as a cook and lived temporarily in the storeroom of the restaurant. Bergman Mendoza was a tall, classically handsome young Latin man who had come to the Crescent City from Nicaragua. He was the headwaiter and sent money back home to help support his grandmother.

As time passed working at Trios, I became good friends with Tony, Daryl, and Bergman. I rented an apartment just below Elysian Fields in an area known as Faubourg Marigny, which along with the Quarter was the original city and the oldest remaining section of New Orleans.

Working as a waiter, to some extent, put my odd convulsions on display. My speech was deteriorating with an exaggerated and accentuated blurting out of words and noises. I became increasingly concerned. The extreme emphasis and de-emphasis of syllables didn't sound exactly like stuttering. It was not a repetition of syllables, rather some syllables were very loud and jerky (like my movements) and others more normal. The result was an awkward lack of fluency in my speech, which took people by surprise. Customers occasionally commented on my so-called nervousness. Most of the time patrons were understanding. One afternoon an older couple had lunch at Trios. After I waited on them, the man said, "We have a daughter about your age who stutters. We think you are doing a great job." I didn't know what to say so I thanked them.

Daryl and Bergman enjoyed taunting each other and

soon I made it a threesome. Daryl would be a mess from cutting, chopping, or mixing a roux in the kitchen, while Bergman was immaculate in dress and grooming, the consummate polished waiter. Daryl would often set Bergman off with his nasty New Orleans tongue, but he was the one with a huge knife in hand and a lot of food to throw. Bergman would chase Daryl around the place throwing things, with Daryl trying to protect himself and usually laughing hysterically. This play repeated itself each day with equal vigor. It is amazing that we remained at Trios for almost the entire year, often venturing out to drink and play pool together after the day's work.

The French Quarter was a place where anything goes, including loud grunts and twitches, and I certainly wanted to take advantage of this. Crowds formed constantly, day and night, on the streets and in bars, with plenty of noise to distract from my own. A few months had passed and I was now living in the center of the Quarter, just off the corner of Royal and St. Peter streets. Sometimes I went out with the conscious decision to engage in whatever interaction came my way and to play it out regardless of where the situation led. I would go the way the wind blew, meeting people on the street—musicians, tap dancers, waitresses—and have an adventure with each one. On one such day, at the A&P, I was greeted by an attractive young woman about my age who came up to me and hugged and kissed me.

"Patrick, how ya doing?" she said. I was agreeable. We talked for a while until our grocery shopping was complete. I suggested to my new acquaintance, Lori, that we go back to my apartment, where we began to make out furiously. I didn't see any harm in it and it felt quite right, so we continued into the afternoon. When I told Lori that I wasn't Patrick she didn't seem very surprised. And I came to the gleeful realization that in sex and matters of the heart, or where the two might meet, I was virtually unaffected by my odd symptoms.

In my quest for adventure I sought out streets and byways to walk that I hadn't previously navigated. Frenchmen Street, just below the Quarter, was right on a park that took up an entire square block. I noticed a pleasant-looking corner building with children playing around it.

"What is this place?" I asked a woman as she left the building.

"It's the Greenhouse. It's a wonderful place," she answered.

I went inside and talked to people there who informed me that the Greenhouse was a short-term home for runaway children. The house seemed full of love and energy, and the counselor suggested I speak to Martin Adamo, who was director of volunteer services. Martin was in charge of screening applicants to the Greenhouse and he invited me to walk around the park.

"We are looking for people interested in volunteering one day a week who will be consistent," he said.

"I have two years of college," I told him, "and in 1976 I worked at a summer camp for emotionally disturbed children near my home in Croton. I like kids, and we seem to get along well." Of course my speech was much interrupted and I continually bobbed my head up and down as if nodding affirmatively. "I'm getting a lot of this," Martin said. He demonstrated my head bobbing and jerking. "What's that about?"

"I guess I'm just nervous," I responded, giving the only explanation I had at the time. Martin told me about a meeting for new volunteers, and shortly after that I began going to the Greenhouse weekly for the next year.

There were a number of people at the Greenhouse whom I admired. Many were excited to be involved in an idealistic cause. One of the social workers, Nancy, was wonderful, smart, pretty, tall, with long black hair, and an offbeat, endearing way about her. She had grown up in

Baltimore and worked as a licensed practical nurse at Charity Hospital during the day. Everyone called her Nurse Nancy. In the evenings she worked at the Greenhouse and studied to become a registered nurse. Nurse Nancy was engaging and interested in learning about people. One afternoon we were having lunch

Volunteering at the Greenhouse, I could easily relate to the children I met there.

on a balcony next to a sixties-style nightclub called the Dream Palace. Nancy was contemplating her future and said she might return to Baltimore. When she asked about my plans I told her that I was thinking about going back to New York and finishing school. "My speech and movements are getting worse," I confided in her. "I'd like to find out what's wrong with me."

And then she said it: "I don't think there is anything really wrong with you. You might have Tourette syndrome."

"What is that?" I asked, never having heard it pronounced, much less explained.

"Tourette is a neurological disorder," she told me. "You should see if there is an organization or something for people who have it."

I didn't know what to make of this information, but as we spoke, a series of flashbacks illuminated in my mind, spotlighting my past history of gyrations and contortions. When I returned to my apartment, I called the Ochsner Clinic, one of the most prestigious hospitals in the south, and asked for the neurology department. The receptionist I spoke to had never heard of Tourette syndrome. I tried the telephone book, looking for any listing under or with "Tourette" in the name, with no success. I felt discouraged yet probably relieved. I could postpone knowing the truth about my condition. It was two years before I heard the word *Tourette* again, a word that would forever change my life.

Since I couldn't find out anything about this neurological disorder I chose to improve my speech. I got a referral to a speech pathologist in a suburb of New Orleans. Money was tight, but the therapy wasn't too expensive, so I made an appointment. I openly explained my speech symptoms to Mary, the young therapist, and she said she could help. Each week we worked on elongating the interval of time I was able to speak fluently, and eventually this enabled me to calm my speech. Diligently practicing the exercises Mary had assigned I was able to greatly improve. I set aside time each week, driving to Metairie where Mary's office was, and had quiet time in my apartment to go over sentences. Although Mary didn't know what was wrong with me I continued with the therapy because she was able to help.

But as my speech returned to normal, a very strange thing happened. Whenever I attempted to stop one symptom or manifestation—like the speech problem—another erupted. Old symptoms were replaced by new tics and gestures, an evolution of symptomatology without reason or warning. I did not realize this is characteristic of Tourette syndrome and sadly unfamiliar to most physicians.

■ ■ ■

One of the most striking experiences I had in New Orleans was at a crowded bar on Bourbon Street. Fascinated I sat and watched an otherwise average-looking man dressed in a suit thrust his whole body forward in a jerky, disruptive motion. He was at the other end of the bar from me.

With his right arm, he clutched his left in an attempt to stop his left arm from thrusting forward. The barmaids were whispering about him. I recall thinking, This guy has the same thing that I have. What the hell is it? The man is much worse than I am, I thought as I observed the barmaids staring at him. Is this how people look at me when I'm having a bad time?

The carnival atmosphere in New Orleans made anything seem possible, even other people with the same problems as me. Through the open door I saw a man with no teeth selling flowers, a small boy tap dancing for dimes, across the street a doorman hawking for customers at a porno palace: "All boys, beautiful boys," he said. Jazz horns echoed through the bar as the crowd became more dense with drinkers. The color and heat of the night began to swell with the liquor. I looked at the man again, still gyrating, pushing and pulling his arms. Some were poking fun at him but in the noise and activity he went mostly unnoticed. I wondered why people make fun of others' misfortunes. I wanted to reach out to this man the way I would to others in ensuing years; instead, I stayed at my end of the bar and finished my drink.

# 3. Diagnosis

At two A.M. in an all-night diner my brother, Evan, and I sat after a long night in the bars. "Lowell, you've got to go to the doctor or a hospital," Evan insisted. "You've got to find out what's wrong with you."

"I don't want to go," I remember saying. "I'll be OK. I know everything will work out."

In 1979, I had returned to New York from New Orleans and I was sharing a Manhattan apartment with Evan. There were two compelling reasons for my return: the first was to finish college and the second was to find out what was wrong with me. But these two motives were also entwined. I had spent the year traveling and working in New Orleans because I thought it was possible to "solve" my problem alone, without help, and "cure" myself of this odd behavior. My symptoms were increasingly frequent and obvious at this time. My head jerked all over the place, my arms thrust out from my body. I stomped my leg deliberately and repeatedly. My Tourette was expressing itself mostly in these ever-present physical punctuations, but I also made involuntary noises, like a periodic grunting sound.

Even though I didn't want to go to a hospital, Evan's words haunted me: "Find out what's wrong with you." While in my teens I first began to experience interrupted and accentuated speech, which sounded like stuttering, the words forced or blurted out in a violent disruption. My mother asked our doctor if my allergies could be the cause. I don't think she actually believed this but was searching, as everyone else was, for an explanation of my bizarre behavior. Just a few of the explanations my family and I suspected for my actions were allergies, nerves, lack of control, hunger, irritability, and anger. For sixteen years my parents had taken me to doctors, insisting something was clearly wrong. Family therapy was advised when my parents explained my symptoms. Therapy would last a number of months or a year, and I'd give up until the next time my symptoms became worse. I often stormed out of the therapist's office, never to return, and my parents were the ones who ended up in counseling. The mental health therapists inevitably blamed

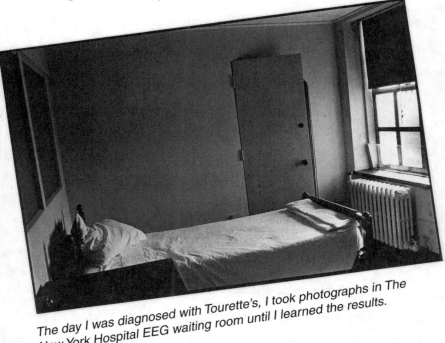

The day I was diagnosed with Tourette's, I took photographs in The New York Hospital EEG waiting room until I learned the results.

my parents, my upbringing, or some aspect of our family environment.

For years I had been fooling myself that my symptoms would go away even though people gawked when I let out one of my loud grunts. I didn't want to stand out in a crowd like this. I felt as if I was being punished by constant humiliation. If I could come to grips with some elusive inner demon that was strangling me, I thought, I would be able to imagine myself miraculously "cured." If I could resolve my problems, then my calmer, more "normal" self would emerge as if from a cocoon.

Months later, before I returned to college for my senior year, I found myself sitting with my parents in the office of Michael Sacks, a psychiatrist at Payne Whitney Clinic at The New York Hospital. "We kept imploring, pleading with you to go to the doctor," my mother recalls. "I think what finally worked was that I told you that you might have a brain tumor. Not for a minute did I believe this, but I thought it was scary enough that it might make you go to the doctor." It only took a couple of visits, including a complete verbal history, before Dr. Sacks said, "You definitely have some kind of Tourette syndrome. You should see a specialist." Then he added, "You're going to have this thing for the rest of your life."

I was both stunned and relieved to find out that my condition had a name. I learned that like me hundreds of thousands of people in this country have Tourette, but I was disheartened by the fact that it would never go away.

"I found the diagnosis devastating," my mother explained to me recently. Most of the time my mother is businesslike in her dealings with people, as opposed to my father's more relaxed, informal demeanor. Her reaction to my diagnosis was one of concern and fear. "I thought it was the end of your world, your future," she recalls. "I remember asking myself, What limitations will he have, what will he be able to do in life?"

My mother had had extensive training as a mental health professional and the diagnosis was confusing and disturbing to her. "On some level I had suspected Tourette syndrome," she says, "and I tried to repress it. I did not believe that you were emotionally disturbed, as was the youngster in a case study I was familiar with." She had continued to insist to herself that I was "normal" except for my quirky behaviors. When Tourette was diagnosed she began to remember the symptoms from when I was very young. "I didn't want to admit to myself or others that you had what was then considered a psychiatric disorder," she says. "I had shut the door on any suspicion of abnormality and now it had crept into our lives anyway."

My father also remembers the news of my diagnosis as devastating. "My world crashed when I got back to the office," he remembers. "I shut my door and put my head on the desk and didn't come out for three days. Putting a name to it fixed it in my mind, that you couldn't get over this. That's what took me down—this was lifelong. It isn't like you can get cured." He thought simply, *That's it.*

My father is a short and compact man; there is not much extra baggage. His face, speckled with a tightly cropped white beard, speaks of age and experience. The skin on his face is pale, with a touch of pink. He is broad shouldered and fit. Since my discovery of Tourette I have wondered if my father has some aspect of the condition too. He has a very calm attitude but makes a constant stream of sounds. I'd hear him whistling old tunes that would sometimes reach frenetic speeds. There was a nervousness in Dad's singing and whistling, even though it's restrained. If he's not singing or whistling he might erupt in a cacophony of throat clearing, nervous rhythm-making, or cheek inflating and deflating. In spite of this, he appears a man in total control, as if even an earthquake would not disturb him. Maybe this quiet hyperactivity is somehow linked to my Tourette. I'll never know for certain. And although scientists now believe there is a strong genetic component in Tourette, it is unclear which gene is involved and thus no genetic testing for couples has been developed.

Was this seeming inability to control words and actions inherited by me, simply in another form? I have learned that obsessive-compulsive behavior is an extended symptom of Tourette. Obsession refers to repetitive, difficult to control, annoying, and sometimes even frightening thoughts. An obsessive thought can be disruptive if it will not go away and if it represents something unpleasant. Some Touretters cannot stop intrusive thoughts of sickness or death, or perhaps thinking illness or death will result from not completing an action like checking to see if the lights are off, or if a symmetrical arrangement of objects is not neatly in place.

Compulsions are actions that cannot be controlled or interrupted. Many people with the full-blown mental illness known as obsessive-compulsive disorder (OCD) feel negative consequences will result if a specific action is not completed. People with Tourette may have OCD in addition to Tourette, or simply, like me, have aspects of their neurological disorder that manifest themselves as thoughts and actions that are difficult to control. Touretters and people with OCD have told me stories about having to dress in a particular sequence and if they don't they feel they must undress and begin again. Checking to see if appliances are turned off is common, as is avoiding cracks on the sidewalk. A typical compulsion is an irrational fear of being touched, or in some cases, such as mine, a desire to touch repeatedly. Excessive hand washing and the need to repeatedly check to see if the house lights are off are other common compulsions.

I know a woman with OCD who thinks continually of the word *Ebola*. Regardless of what is happening around her in conversations or on the television or radio, she is thinking Ebola. The fact that the word represents a horrible, deadly virus does not matter to her; more significant is the sound the word makes audibly and in her mind when it's repeated. She is fascinated by the "acoustic contours" of the word itself. Touretters often develop such an obsession with words, lost in an amusement park of the mind where they can spend hours turning over the vocal and mental variations in form, inflection, pitch, and even the meaning of a word or phrase. A single word may become the roller-coaster ride for a Touretter on which he or she can be carried away for hours, unable to complete another task.

I now realize many of my family members have some type of obsessive personality. My mother might mention something she wants to say five or six times in a conversation, repeatedly making her point over and over again. My aunt and uncle are also compulsive people, sometimes ballooning to a weight of three hundred pounds apiece. I suspect if food was put in front of my aunt and uncle they would be compelled to finish the plate, regardless of how much was prepared. They both have the same insistent way of talking that my mother has, so no matter how many times something is said, it is never finished.

Once the diagnosis of Tourette was made, everything began to fall into place. Memories of actions I previously thought unconnected now fit the profile of this new reality. The way my head jerked and bobbed, both from side to side and up and down, in a very rapid twitching was a classic Tourettism. Sometimes it caused a headache. I was also prone to deliberate eye blinking, my eyes squeezed together in an exaggerated grimace.

After hearing the report from my doctor, I found myself reexamining my life as a history of this disorder. I now saw in my childhood actions early obsessive-compulsive traits, if not the full-blown tics of Tourette. Another strange "habit" I developed when I was older was to take the sharpened point of a pencil and thrust it downward all over a piece of paper so that it was completely pockmarked. Each time I thought I was finished, concluding a kind of fit that

I hoped was ebbing, I'd experience another flurry of paper poking.

Early in my teens when I got my first camera, I walked around throwing this expensive piece of equipment in the air and catching it before it fell. Despite my father's warning, "You're going to drop it," I couldn't stop. When I began listening to rock-and-roll music, my father would often ask me to lower the volume. In response I would have to turn the stereo up really loud before I turned it lower. I had to feel the volume knob touch its maximum level before I returned it to a lower volume. Like others with Tourette, I felt a tactile satisfaction gained from accomplishing these acts.

One incident that stands out as extreme, even in my experience, took place in my parents' well-maintained suburban home. I was an avid photography enthusiast even in high school, and one of my most valued pieces of equipment was a beautiful steel tripod. My father recalls that I had gone to my room very frustrated about something. When he came home from work, my mother said, "Let me show you what Lowell did this time." Every tabletop in the house already had holes in it as I had knifed them to death. But this time I had made holes with my tripod in the wall in my room.

As I got older, I grew increasingly frustrated, usually at my inability to read or write, and one day as a storm brewed inside me I lifted the tripod over my head and threw it through the wall. After many weeks of this my father informed me that if I continued smashing the walls he was going to take the tripod and smash it over the stone wall that surrounded our house. Sure enough, when my father saw what I had done, he took the tripod and simply smashed the shit out of it. Then he returned it to me and said, "The next time you do this, I'll do this to the camera." To many people my father's reaction may seem violent and extreme, but my behavior had been violent, too. He was simply trying to find a way to counter my own violence, perhaps to shock me out of it. As he later put it, "a little light went on in your head and you never did it again."

Now that I had a diagnosis, I wanted to see if anything could be done about my condition. I wanted to confide in people I trusted, to explain my new situation. I called Lisette Model, a friend and mentor and one of the most influential photographers of the century. She lived across town from Evan and me in Greenwich Village and I used to go out to dinner with Lisette about once a month. "I found out what I have," I told her at one of our dinners, "why I make these jerky movements. I've got Tourette syndrome."

Lisette's response startled me. "Of course, darling," she said. "I heard on the television, if you do this kind of thing, and have that kind of movement, then you have this thing." When I asked her why she hadn't talked to me about it, she said, "You can't tell someone they have something wrong with them. They have to learn it for themselves." In fact, it had taken me more than twenty years to learn about Tourette, and there was much more I would learn in the months and years to come.

■  ■  ■

At the time of my diagnosis I had returned to school as a senior at School of Visual Arts in New York. It was very difficult to concentrate on schoolwork with what was going on in my life. I was depressed and often had periods of sleep and despair. During that semester I was photographing a degenerate portrait of New York in the subways and the subjects mirrored my feelings of melancholy.

My instructor at the time was an antagonistic man with little humor. Jim took no excuse for lack of motivation on his students' part and graded me poorly in his class. I

On Avenue A in New York's East Village, I caught a glimpse of an old woman whose despair mirrored my own.

contested my grade but his decision was final. Despite my difficulty, I graduated from School of Visual Arts with a bachelor's degree in photography.

I was to have another run-in with this instructor two years later at a gallery opening. I often volunteered at this gallery, which sponsored traveling exhibitions and workshops teaching photography to prison inmates and other disadvantaged groups. One spring evening I was attending an opening for such an exhibition. Lisette had just died and I was sharing the loss with other colleagues when I encountered Jim at the party. As the group dispersed later that evening, he came up to me screaming, inexplicably furious at what I thought he must have perceived as a challenge to order. "Lowell," he confronted me in a rage, "you're hiding behind your illness." Jim stood there with his fists clenched, his chest inflated. "I'm calling you a shithead," he challenged, "now you throw the first punch. I'm calling you a shithead, now what are you going to do about it?"

I was scared of this guy and wanted no part of getting into a fight with him. I got into my car and drove away. I knew Jim had no idea what my illness was but was probably looking to pick a fight due to his own insecurities. I wondered what was going on inside his mind. I thought his reaction to my behavior was very bizarre, to say the least.

Jim's response stood in stark contrast to the attitude of another one of my instructors. During my final year at School of Visual Arts I took a photography class taught by Dennis Simonetti, who explained in his opening lecture that he was suffering from his own neurological disorder. Dennis had recently been diagnosed with Parkinson's disease. He demonstrated the tremors in his hands and asked his students not to be alarmed because this was an involuntary movement due to his illness. As Dennis and I got to know each other, he asked me what type of nervous disorder I had, and though he had never heard of Tourette before, he accepted my explanation instantly. (Interestingly, Parkinson's disease is the result of a deficiency of dopamine, while Tourette reflects an excess of dopamine activity. I realized later that Dennis's brain and mine would be in perfect balance.) Dennis was a brilliant photographer and printer. I learned a great deal from him—not only about photography—and we became good friends.

From my experiences with Jim and Dennis, I recognized the two extremes. Two individuals reacted to me and my disorder in totally different ways. One person was threatened, the other compassionate. In general, I have come to realize that the scope of reaction to my behavior falls into one of three categories: fear, sympathy, or indifference. I noticed that people who were especially nervous or uncomfortable with themselves were most bothered by my Tourette, as if they were internalizing my disorder. People in close proximity to me sometimes commented that they thought I was mocking them.

■ ■ ■

It took time for me to come to grips with Tourette syndrome. I was relieved to know that I had it, to know I wasn't alone, and that many, many people experience the same feelings. I had even come to know what to expect when people encountered me or I told them about the disorder. But I was also afraid. While Tourette was not a fatal or degenerative condition, it was different every day. I never knew what form it would take, and when.

What was worse was that every twitch or noise I made was an opportunity for someone to comment on my behavior. One morning I went out to buy a newspaper and a cup of coffee at a corner store, a hub of activity at St. Mark's Place and Second Avenue. While buying the newspaper a panhandler on the corner looked at me as I was grunting and twitching and commented, "Been hitting the vodka again, eh, buddy?" I would begin the day already angry and feeling that if anyone said anything to me I'd be mad enough to hit them in the face. There were times when I felt ready to detonate, an explosion waiting to happen. Once a stranger and I crossed paths on Second Avenue and the man began to mock me, imitating my loud noises, as if I were doing it on purpose. I made the noise repeatedly, and the man repeated it as well. I wanted to take my hands and ring that man's neck until every breath was gone from his body. But I didn't. I went on about my business. During these angry periods I felt it was dangerous just to leave the apartment.

I had learned that there was a national organization, the Tourette Syndrome Association, located in Bayside, New York, but I was afraid to meet other people with this condition. I was afraid that I might see how much worse the disorder could be, or that I would in fact become worse somehow through this contact, as if Tourette were contagious, even to a Touretter. It was a full year before I joined the association and began attending occasional meetings. Even though I had always thought of myself as somewhat "different," I never thought of myself as "damaged" or "abnormal" in any way. Once I had been told I had a disorder—once labeled, in effect—I began to see things in terms of "them" and "us." In most basic respects, I was an average guy, but now I was slightly defective, an outsider to society.

Would I be able to continue my career in photography? Would I become some kind of village idiot, living out my life in solitude and distress? Would I ever have a remission? Would it ever go away? How would I be able to function socially or professionally? Would women shun me? The future might bring uncontrollable cursing, worse symptoms or better symptoms, disability or remission. I had no idea and no way yet to figure out what this thing meant to me.

# 4. Drugs and Orphan Drugs

After my diagnosis, I made an appointment with a neurologist at The New York Hospital that would lead to my long and complex relationship with drugs. The doctor explained to me that my symptoms could be made manageable with a prescription of 3 milligrams a day of haloperidol, known by its trade name Haldol. Haldol is a psychotropic medication affecting certain chemicals in the brain called neurotransmitters that influence a wide variety of behaviors. It is suspected that people with Tourette have an overabundance of dopamine, which is responsible for the ability to control and inhibit movement. Haldol reduces the amount of dopamine released at the synapse, or gap, between brain receptors, thus lessening dopamine's effects.

Once Haldol was prescribed for me, I immediately felt relief from my tics. During the first two or three weeks of taking the medication I was elated by this newfound normalcy and the feeling of "fitting in." But Haldol, like any drug, has potentially dangerous short- and long-term side effects, to which I was not immediately alerted. Within two or three weeks of taking the drug, I was plagued by a gnawing hunger and mental dulling. At times I'd have a fidgety restlessness, and then I'd experience the reverse—a zombielike state of lethargy and depression.

I began reading medical journals in search of an alternative medication. Through my activity in the Tourette Syndrome Association I met Abbey Meyers, who has three children with Tourette. Abbey was director of patient services for the association and had put together a wealth of information about medication and the pharmaceutical industry. In my research I came across material on pimozide (Orap), which is very similar to Haldol but has fewer side effects. I found that one doctor was repeatedly mentioned in connection with virtually all current research: Arthur K. Shapiro. Dr. Shapiro had authored a book on the medical aspects of Tourette syndrome, as well as numerous scientific papers. It wasn't until years later that I learned Shapiro was largely responsible for Tourette syndrome being thought of as an organic neurological disorder rather than a psychiatric illness. Dr. Shapiro was a psychiatrist, but he helped develop a new physiological outlook on the disorder. After years of misinformation and psychodynamic thought connected to the mere mention of Tourette syndrome, the seventies brought a return to the original, long-forgotten hypothesis about the disorder.

In 1885, the French physician Dr. Gilles de la Tourette published a paper describing six individuals with chronic multiple tics which he believed to be an organic disorder. Tourette, who was a student of the famous neurologist Jean-Martin Charcot, described a condition almost exactly as we have come to view it today:

"Although the movements can vary in their form from one individual to another, they still maintain general characteristics which are the same in all subjects. One of these characteristics is the abruptness with which the movements appear and another is their rapidity. Suddenly and without warning, a grimace or contortion appears once, twice, or several times. Then all is quiet. But soon afterward (for generally the intervals between movements are quite close) new jerks appear. Importantly, most of these movements are limited either to the face, an extremity, or a combination of these two. In the latter case, the movements are usually more frequent and intense."

In this landmark paper, Dr. Gilles de la Tourette quotes one of his patients, "an intelligent twenty-four-year-old man," who commented: "In listening to a discussion I was seized by the almost irresistible need to repeat a word or the end of a sentence. I needed all my strength and sense of propriety to hold back from repeating this word out loud; as I could only restrain myself part way. I saw on different occasions how people around me clearly heard my noises."

Now, almost a hundred years later, Abbey Meyers helped put me in touch with a modern-day physician who also saw Tourette as a *physical* complaint. I made an appointment to visit Dr. Shapiro on Manhattan's Upper East Side.

Dr. Shapiro was a diminutive man with white hair and had what might be considered a gruff bedside manner. Many, including myself, were put off by what seemed to be a disrespectful demeanor. Actually, he was an extremely dedicated scientist who was uneasy with people. At first I felt he was uncaring and insensitive, but I later realized he was working to help all those who have Tourette in a broad, all-encompassing sense, not just individually.

Dr. Shapiro sat behind a huge modern desk saying little and occasionally putting up his hand to stop me from talking unnecessarily. In keeping with his role as modern psychiatrist turned pharmacologist, his shelves and windowsills displayed an exhibition of historical paraphernalia, including mortar and pestle. The doctor instructed me to keep careful charts, which he provided, to record my symptom reduction in relation to side effects incurred by each drug he administered. Unlike the neurologist at The New York Hospital who picked a dosage at random and said goodbye, Dr. Shapiro began my treatment with Haldol at a minuscule dose. It was increased in tiny increments, very gradually, until I hit a wall of side effects. Using this system, known as titration, a maximum therapeutic effect was reached with a minimum of side effects. Once this level was attained a second drug, Cogentin, was given to relieve side effects from the Haldol.

A few months later I questioned Dr. Shapiro about his use of the drug pimozide, which I had read about. The doctor was administering Orap, the trade name for the drug, through the Investigational New Drug Program, even though it had not yet been approved by the Food and

Drug Administration. The IND Program, as it was known, gave doctors a way to prescribe new medications under consideration by the FDA before actual approval. One of the benefits to the patient was use of the medicine without the cost of a prescription. Pimozide had been available in Europe and Canada for years, but mostly for use with schizophrenic patients in significantly higher doses.

Dr. Shapiro agreed we would try the drug. Pimozide worked well for me, with slightly better symptom relief and no side effects. Although the exact mode of action has not been established, doctors speculate that pimozide probably blocks a different set of dopamine receptors than Haldol. I was to see Dr. Shapiro once every three months, to monitor medication and go over the records I kept. In addition, I was required to have complete blood work done twice a year. This visit to Arthur Shapiro became a ritual I both looked forward to and dreaded. In the back of my mind I always worried something might go wrong, that the relief I had begun to feel might prove to be a momentary respite before my symptoms returned, more pronounced than ever.

■ ■ ■

In November 1983, Abbey Meyers phoned me asking if I would accompany her to Washington, D.C. "When there is controversy about a drug like pimozide, the FDA will sometimes hold a public hearing on its approval," she explained. "They allow public input, which means we can testify."

Abbey is a woman with a fire in her belly. She was with the association when her three children were young and she was determined to find better approaches to their treatment. They have grown up and adjusted well to adulthood in spite of Tourette. Abbey founded and is currently executive director of the National Organization for Rare Disorders (NORD). She discussed with me how patients can effect change in their treatment from pharmaceutical companies and government agencies. "People with the rare disease voluntary agencies began to understand that if scientists ever came up with an answer, some kind of treatment, it wouldn't be manufactured if it was for too small a market."

Abbey recounted the events that led up to this FDA hearing. "My son was taking pimozide, we were going to Dr. Arthur Shapiro. He was doing very well on pimozide and we went back for our three-month visit, at which time the doctor would normally give us a three-month supply of the drug. This time Dr. Shapiro gave us the three-month supply, but said he couldn't give it to us any longer because the company was stopping the manufacture of the drug." It turned out that the manufacturer was really developing the drug for a more prevalent condition, schizophrenia, which affects 4 to 5 million Americans. But when it became evident that pimozide was not very effective for schizophrenia and the only other condition for which it was a possible treatment is Tourette, with far fewer potential customers, they were stopping the manufacture and availability of the drug in the United States.

"I called the FDA and tried to get some answers," Abbey recalls, "but they wouldn't talk to me. No matter what the FDA knows, drug formulas are considered a trade secret, and they are simply not allowed to talk to ordinary consumers even to let them know the status of the debate. I began talking to other voluntary health agencies. Some of them had similar problems with drugs for their disease. Some drugs were being made by hand by academic scientists in their laboratory because no commercial company was interested in manufacturing them."

Abbey would not be dissuaded. "Then I spoke to Majorie Guthrie." (Woody Guthrie, the famed folksinger who died of Huntington's disease, was Majorie's husband, and folksinger Arlo's father.) "Majorie was the founder of the Committee to Combat Huntington's Disease. She said she cared very much about this subject because even though they didn't have a treatment for Huntington's, someday there would be. She wanted to make sure that when the day comes the drug would be manufactured. At this same time Adam Ward Seligman [a young man with Tourette syndrome from California] was getting pimozide from Canada and asked a friend to bring

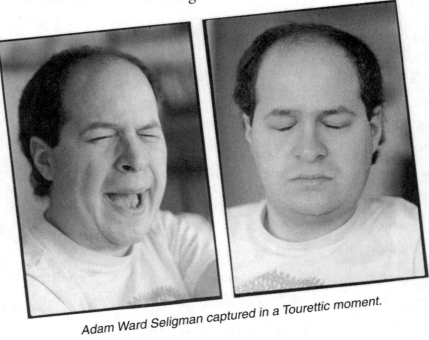

*Adam Ward Seligman captured in a Tourettic moment.*

back a supply. Customs stopped this man and confiscated the pimozide. Adam's mother, Muriel, called me and asked what she should do. I told her to go to her congressman, who very conveniently turned out to be

Henry Waxman, the chairman of the House subcommittee on Health and the Environment. When Waxman found out this was a problem he decided to call hearings about what drugs fell into this 'limited' category. Adam and I testified, as did Dr. Van Woert, who was making a drug for myoclonus [a form of epilepsy] by hand in his laboratory."

When Abbey asked me to help her testify, the thought that I could contribute something to the course of medical history was difficult to believe. Instead of feeling like a victim, perhaps I could take this opportunity and initiative toward change. I remember sleeping overnight at Abbey's house in Connecticut so we could fly to Washington at dawn the next morning. Abbey's children were there readying themselves for Halloween. I also met her husband and got a sense of the remarkable sacrifices the family had made in order to facilitate this crusade to make things better for their children, and for all of us. Abbey traveled two hours each morning from her home to the offices of the Tourette Syndrome Association in Queens. She was constantly flying somewhere on association business, often requiring days away from home.

I dressed in a suit that morning, a rarity for me, for my trip to the Capitol. The flight out of New York's La Guardia Airport was filled with businessmen reading the *New York*

*Times* and the *Washington Post*. On the hour-long flight, I wondered what would await us at the FDA. During this trip, I felt more free to Tourette because we were on a mission. When I am on a plane, I become fixated on the seat in front of mine and how hard I can kick it without disturbing the passenger sitting there. It becomes almost like a game, a game that I cannot control. As I grunted and kicked the seat in front of mine, I imagined explaining our trip to any disgruntled passenger who inquired. If Tourette is without reason, on this trip at least my disorder had a purpose.

After we landed in Washington, Abbey and I took a cab to Rockville, Maryland, the headquarters of the Food and Drug Administration. We met Dr. Shapiro there and entered a huge room filled with people talking around a U-shaped table equipped with microphones. In another section of the room was the press with tape recorders and notepads, just waiting for the conclusions that would come out of this event. A standing mike and podium were at the far end of the room where I would be asked to tell a little bit about myself and why I felt pimozide should be approved. We sat and listened to the members of the Psycho-pharmacological Advisory Committee discuss the attributes and problems with pimozide for hours. Some of the data showed heart problems with high doses of the drug and the committee was concerned. The doctors on the committee also wanted to be certain about the efficacy of the drug. Dr. Shapiro and Abbey had testified. Finally, it was time for me to speak. I got up and walked to the microphone.

"My name is Lowell Handler, I'm twenty-seven years old, and I've been taking pimozide for almost two years now. When I began treatment with haloperidol, I experienced side effects that were very difficult for me. Once I began with pimozide I had no side effects and better symptom reduction. I hope everyone here today will vote to approve pimozide, in order to give those of us who need it a better chance."

It seemed I had come a long way to say so little. Before I knew it I was back in my seat next to Abbey, to listen to hours more discussion. The reporters were writing furiously; during a break some of them asked me questions.

At the end of a nine-hour day the Psychopharmacological Advisory Committee to the Food and Drug Administration recommended the FDA commissioner approve pimozide. Hundreds of people in the room applauded. I felt relieved the day was over and satisfied that individuals can make a difference in a system. A couple of months later pimozide was available in pharmacies around the country.

Not only is the drug available by prescription, but the manufacturer helps educate doctors about its use with Tourette. Prior to FDA approval, no drug with the strength and effectiveness of Haldol but with fewer side effects was available in this country.

Pimozide was one of the first drugs to be approved under the Orphan Drug Act, which later became law. A so-called orphan drug is for a disease that affects two hundred thousand Americans or less. As Abbey had told me, a huge drug company was not going to "adopt" one of these orphans without the financial benefits that the Orphan Drug Act provided because it wouldn't be profitable.

The Orphan Drug Act created a series of tax incentives to entice drug companies to develop drugs for rare diseases for small populations of people. The act also provided a surrogate patent law, so for seven years the pharmaceutical company responsible for developing the drug had no competition from "generic" manufacturers. Previous to this act of Congress, a "generic" manufacturer could immediately compete in the marketplace. This combined with a fifty-cent tax exemption for each dollar spent on clinical research, provided the drug companies with drastically reduced costs and increased profits. Ironically, even though pimozide was one of the initial drugs that helped result in the passage of the Orphan Drug Act, it never was officially designated as an orphan drug. Even before the Orphan Drug Act was enforced, the manufacturer of pimozide agreed to make the drug available in order to stop bad publicity resulting from the pharmaceutical industry's opposition to government regulation, and thus opposition to the Orphan Drug Act. Each time the act was cited in the press, pimozide was given as an example of how new medications could be made available.

I recently spoke with Abbey and was curious to hear where she thought her groundbreaking work with the Orphan Drug Act was leading us today. I mentioned the Clinton health care plan, which I thought was a great step in the right direction but failed because of lobbying by the insurance companies that had the most to lose if the plan was a success.

"The situation has to get to a point where healthy people feel threatened by it," Abbey argued. "Right now it's only people like you and my family, or people who have experienced serious health problems, who understand how desperate the health care system is. People don't realize they can be hurt at any time, especially young people who think they can do anything: climb mountains and fly on bungee ropes without getting injured. Until the healthy voter understands that he is vulnerable to serious illness there will not be the political willpower to do something about our health care situation in the United States. The rest of the industrialized world passed these laws in the early part of the century. We are a century behind the rest of the world."

Abbey has worked tirelessly on reform, but she feels there is something in the American character—a selfishness—that is to blame for our politics.

"We as Americans have not begun to face our responsibility to care for each other," Abbey said. "You think it won't happen to you. You care about yourself or your neighbor, but not anyone beyond your community. We've got to share the expense of chronic illness."

■ ■ ■

My conversations with Abbey made me wonder if we as a society are guilty of what a friend of mine called the "arrogance of good health." It seems that we are divided into opposite camps of "them" and "us." Perhaps people with no health problems do not want to be exposed to, or even have knowledge of, those who do, for fear they might somehow be affected. The orphan drug movement is very important to our health care crisis, and as Abbey pointed out, "It is becoming worldwide." Japan passed an Orphan

Drug Act about three years ago, and the European Community is about to pass one now. Diseases are less rare when looked at on a global basis. Recently I watched Abbey spar with a leader in the health insurance industry on public television's *McNeil/Lehrer Newshour*. Seeing this segment in a national prime-time broadcast made me hopeful that perhaps the time has come when people can hear as clearly as Abbey has had the vision and determination to see.

# 5. <u>Life</u> and Leukemia

**I** **have always been much more comfortable with shapes and colors than with letters or words.** Growing up with dyslexia I had a difficult time interpreting words in print. I wanted to capture part of the world, as seen through my eyes, in black and white. I discovered that all I had to do was freeze something or someone in time and space.

Photographing is an exhilarating experience for me. I am involved, an observer and a participant at the same time. It is difficult to write about photography or talk about it much, because the act is experiential and proactive. Photography is an act of commentary, political activism, journalism, or social defiance. When photography communicates emotionally it transcends the act and becomes an art. After I complete a day's assignment, I feel satisfied, as if I have really accomplished something.

After my parents bought me my first 35mm camera on my thirteenth birthday, I began to photograph everything. I spent hours, days, looking at old *Life* magazines from the fifties and sixties, and lying in bed at night I tried to imagine myself in an exotic location working for the great picture magazine. My grades were poor in high school; not able to read or write very well, I was accepted at Emerson College, a Boston liberal arts college based on a portfolio of photographs.

I knew after that first year of college I'd need to greatly improve my photographic skills to compete in an overcrowded field where magazines have one assignment for a thousand photographers. But I had also wasted a lot of time partying and socializing during that first year in Boston. If high school was difficult due to a lack of acceptance by my peers, college was pleasantly the opposite. It seemed like anything was acceptable, even twitching, especially in the seventies when long hair and the drug-influenced counterculture were in fashion. Nothing was too far out, and in this anything-goes atmosphere I felt at home. The excitement of being at Emerson, in a big city,

Through my work at Camp Rainbow, a community for so-called emotionally disturbed children, I began to find a kind of beauty in disorder.

with people my age constantly around, whet my appetite for an even bigger city with more stimulation. I wanted to be in the thick of the art world, and I transferred to a major photography department at School of Visual Arts in New York City, where I was again accepted based on my portfolio. During that summer I worked as a counselor at a camp for so-called emotionally disturbed children. Using a small Leica camera and only one lens, I made portraits of these children to communicate their isolation and poetic beauty.

Our school was visited by the editors of *Popular Photography*, who were running a series called "Pop Photo on Campus." They chose about a half-dozen candidates from over two thousand students—including me. Later that same year, *U.S. Camera* magazine published an eight-page portfolio of my photographs from the summer camp. I was nineteen years old, and elated that my career had begun. My photographs were reaching an audience.

After these early successes in publishing, I still did not know how to make a living with my work. It was an advantage to be able to work alone and not around other people in an office. As a photographer I could make my own schedule and work independently, but I worried that I wouldn't be given a chance due to my "problem." I wanted to become a photojournalist, but people were put off by my symptoms.

■ ■ ■

After I finished college I left the apartment Evan and I shared in New York City and moved to Cold Spring, a small town an hour north. I spent several years at short-lived jobs as a waiter, cook, office assistant, counselor, gardener, cleanup man, and liquor store stock boy. In between and during all these jobs I practiced my craft in the hopes of landing some paid work as a photographer.

In photojournalism there are two key elements one must have to be hired: access and location. The axiom of the business is "f 8 and be there," which means have the correct lens setting and be at the right place at the right time. If there is one thing I have access to it's Tourette syndrome, I thought, so why not photograph a story on someone with the disorder? A published piece would educate and illuminate at least some aspect of Tourette. Perhaps if I had seen such a piece I would have recognized my own condition sooner.

At this time I had an old friend who was a journalist freelancing for *Time-Life* magazines. In the fall of 1984, Caroline called me to say she remembered seeing the series of photographs I had done of emotionally disturbed children. She asked me if I would be interested in doing something like that for *Life*. As calmly as I could, I said yes. I then suggested to her that a story on people with Tourette syndrome hadn't been done before. We put together our approach and wrote a query letter to the science editor at the magazine. Waiting for the response felt like an eternity. When it came, I found it hard to believe. They were interested in a picture story: a series of photographs with limited text or extended captions. This was, of course, my dream.

The editors instructed me I'd have to begin the project on my own, with no commitment or money from *Life* until I proved the story feasible. It was a hardship working for no money, but I did this in the hopes of being hired. They asked me to pitch a variety of story ideas about people in various situations who have Tourette so we could choose a plan. I had a good working relationship by now with the Tourette Syndrome Association, attending meetings and helping to develop local chapters. The groups that formed the association were in part social, and parents especially were eager to exchange information about behavior and medication. I contacted the association and explained the project. Luckily they were eager to help and gave me the names of people in the area. I decided to focus on Art

Bailey, a man about my age in New York City with fairly severe Tourette.

The challenge was to show the syndrome photographically—in still images. Before I began to photograph Art, I asked a friend to pose for me, imitating jerky Tourettic movements in a darkened

room while

Using modern photographic techniques, I captured, for the first time, this series of portraits of the Tourettic experience.

I photographed using Polaroid film and a strobe (or electronic flash). I worked out an exposure, leaving the shutter open for a full minute and popping the strobe at approximately twenty-second intervals. These three overlapping images created a dramatic collage, freezing the subject while going through a Tourettic episode. Since the session was accomplished in total darkness the only images registering on the film were those taken when the strobe flashed. In this way, I gauged the exposure and was ready to begin a first-time-ever story about a man with Tourette. I went to Art's house at night and photographed for hours, producing one perfect roll of pictures, each frame in the sequence they were taken. I submitted this enlarged contact sheet to John Loengard, the picture editor at *Life*.

Loengard was a legendary staff photographer at *Life* from the 1950s until the magazine folded in the early seventies. When *Life* reemerged in 1979, it was with Loengard as picture editor. John is a large man, known for giving beginning photographers like me a shot at the big time. I was called in to see John the day I submitted my first pictures and was told the assignment was a go.

His office was cluttered with years of old *Life* magazines, notes, and photo books. "This looks like my apartment," I said, as we shook hands. I had to contain my excitement. Up to this moment I hadn't had one magazine assignment, and now I was working for *Life* with one of the most renowned photographers in the business. John and I discussed various aspects of the story, whom I should photograph and how, along with fees and some of the logistics.

"You've got the assignment," John said. "If the other people you are going to photograph are as expressive as this guy, you'll get some good shots."

The hard part was yet to come—who else would I photograph and what would the story be? John and I discussed this and decided I should begin by contacting Abbey Myers and explain what we were looking for. "Someone who is very successful, and has the patience of a saint," I said.

I wanted to show someone with Tourette who could function on a high level, even with the difficulties the disorder presented. Abbey told me about Orrin Palmer, a medical school student with severe Tourette. Orrin was enrolled in New York Medical College, located in Valhalla, just north of the city. Orrin's first response to my phone call was one of disbelief. He wanted the name and phone number of the editor at *Life* to verify that I really was on assignment. A few days later we began a telephone dialogue and finally met one night in a local bar. Orrin, who lived with his fiancée, Jill, was intelligent and captivating. His serious demeanor belied an offbeat, and sometimes raunchy, sense of humor.

He was about my age and had gone through many trials with medication. Orrin's symptoms were somewhat atypical in that he would strike a movement or pose and then apparently freeze for a few seconds, which was quite bizarre to witness. He found his patients significantly more tolerant than many of his medical colleagues.

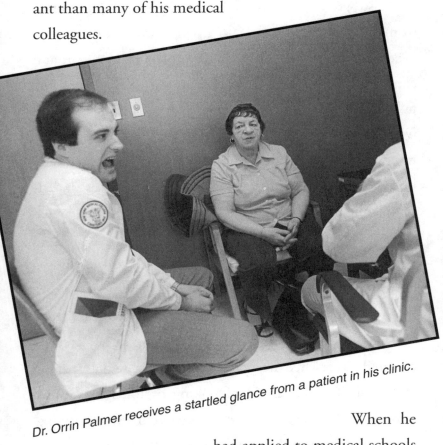

Dr. Orrin Palmer receives a startled glance from a patient in his clinic.

When he had applied to medical schools some places rejected him because of Tourette. Orrin suffered through many years of difficult schooling and discrimination. He also had extreme learning disabilities; Jill read aloud to him many of the texts required for his courses. I immediately felt an affinity and easy friendship with Orrin.

I also grew to know Jill, a strong and determined woman who understood Orrin and every obstacle he needed to overcome. Jill was also protective of Orrin and concerned about how I would portray him. When we talked about the impact Tourette had on her relationship with Orrin, she said, "I just don't notice." This is often the response from someone living with a Touretter. Loved ones become used to involuntary movements and noises, and after a while it almost seems natural. I've noticed this myself in long-term relationships.

I photographed Orrin and Jill over a full year, including on rounds at the hospital, accompanying colleagues, examining patients, and, finally, graduating from medical school.

One of Orrin's most difficult situations, he later recounted, was when he had to examine a female patient seminude. He was afraid of poking or touching her inappropriately. Although people are often understanding, situations can arise that are difficult and embarrassing. Orrin told me he had to explain Tourette to patients to put them at ease. Once, during an examination, Orrin poked a woman's breast. She was very shocked, and they both couldn't help feeling strange and embarrassed.

Orrin also cursed, and one of his favorite sayings was "Fuck you boy," shouted out in Tourettic fashion. Coprolalia, or involuntary cursing, including racial epithets and derogatory expressions, occurs in about 15 percent of people with Tourette, which scientists attribute to an inability of the brain to inhibit language as well as thought and movement. People with Tourette are not necessarily expressing anger or bigotry but rather saying what one wishes could be repressed. All of these words and expressions are familiar in our society. Any one of us might think something derogatory, but we automatically inhibit ourselves from saying it. I've explained to people that if you were walking down the street and saw a four-hundred-pound person, you might think "fatso." It's doubtful you would blurt out the word, but people with Tourette might not be able to stop themselves. I knew a woman in New York City who had coprolalia and who is also a lesbian. She lived with her parents and was most afraid of them discovering her sexual preference. The one word she blurted out time and time again, loudly, and often, was "gay."

Another Touretter remembers being in line at a bank. An attractive black man was standing in front of her wearing a purple sweater. Over and over she kept repeating to herself "purple nigger, purple nigger," until she actually said it out loud. She felt no racial prejudice toward this man but simply couldn't get out of her mind the one word she knew was most inappropriate to say. Fortunately the man was understanding.

The great thing about Orrin, too, is his sense of humor regarding himself. He knew he couldn't stop from shouting meaningless expressions, but he could joke about it to someone who understood.

*Life* assigns many more stories than those actually published, and unfortunately the piece on Orrin Palmer was passed over for "flashier" subjects. I was deeply disappointed but pushed onward to find an alternative placement for my work. Even though the story didn't run I was paid, and the following year I got in touch with Oliver Sacks at his home on City Island off the Bronx. At this time the famous neurologist's phone number was listed, so I called and introduced myself. I was curious about Dr. Sacks and wanted to see if we might collaborate.

Sacks' book, *The Man Who Mistook His Wife for a Hat,* was a bestseller and included, among other things, stories about people with Tourette syndrome. In one chapter, Sacks describes a drummer, Witty Ticcy Ray, who syncopates his Touretticisms with percussion and takes "drug holidays" from Haldol so he can retain certain aspects of his excessive personality routinely diminished by the medication. In another case, Dr. Sacks discusses a much more severe, phantasmagoric form of "super Tourette's" with a profound effect on a person's identity. According to Oliver, this type of Tourette can almost overwhelm the individual, and even drive him or her into a "Tourette psychosis." This was the first time I remembered reading in a popular book anything about the lives of those with Tourette, and I felt Oliver Sacks' work gave insight and a human face to aspects of a disorder previously unknown to the general public. Before meeting Oliver I wondered what he would be like. Would he be able to unlock the secret of my Tourette or know the spell that would make it disappear?

"I'm the only one photographing Tourette, and you're the only one writing about it," I said during our first encounter. "Maybe we could do something together."

After months of meetings and discussion, it finally seemed as though we were ready to collaborate. At a meeting of the Tourette Syndrome Association we heard about a Mennonite family in northern Canada with several generations affected by Tourette. Oliver and I looked at each other and said, "We've got to go." When the editors at *Life* discovered Oliver and I were working together, they suggested a new project with Oliver as author, and in 1987 we spent three weeks in LaCrete, Alberta, the northernmost farming community on the continent. The resulting photographs and Oliver's text were published in September 1988, and later, through Black Star—an international photography agency—published worldwide.

At the time, Howard Chapnick, a stalwart in the business, ran Black Star and acted as a mentor to many aspiring photojournalists. No subject or location was too remote for a Black Star photographer to capture and I decided to call Chapnick in the hope that he could help me place my story on Orrin Palmer. I knew Chapnick only by reputation and procrastinated for days, expecting to be put off by secretaries and assistants. Finally, I got up my nerve.

"Howard Chapnick, please," I said.

Imagine my surprise when Howard answered his own phone. "Speaking," a firm but friendly voice responded.

When I explained I was a photographer and wanted to show him a portfolio, he said, "I'll see you at ten A.M. on Wednesday."

Chapnick was in his early sixties, not tall yet distinguished in voice and stature. He was inquisitive and businesslike, yet friendly with people. I showed him the story on Orrin Palmer and Tourette syndrome, in addition to a couple of other series I had completed, and he quizzed me about the disorder. I did not know if he was familiar with Tourette. And then he told me, "The pictures are compositionally and technically very good. Maybe I should write about you in my *Popular Photography* column." I was ecstatic. The column ran a few months later and I began a friendship with Howard that lasted long after his retirement. Black Star took the story on Orrin and Tourette and published it in *Hippocrates*, a new general circulation magazine specializing in issues of health and medicine. In later months my story, with Howard's help, was printed in *Moda*, a magazine in Italy, and *Manchette*, a Brazilian publication. After the piece was syndicated, I became a contract photographer for Black Star.

■　■　■

At the same time I was experiencing my first major professional success, my personal life was about to be shattered. It was the evening before my last day's shoot with Orrin and Jill. I was feeling happy that the year-long assignment would be complete. I fantasized about the finished layout being a hit in print. I compared my first magazine piece, in my mind, with the great *Life* stories of the past. Just then the phone interrupted my daydream. It was my brother, Evan, calling from the apartment we had shared and where he still lived.

"Lowell, I'm going into the hospital at nine tomorrow morning. I've got leukemia." I dropped the phone on the floor in shock.

"Lowell." I heard Evan's voice echo from my kitchen floor. He had been complaining for days about a mild rash, feeling weak, and a sore throat. "I went to a doctor; he took blood and ran some tests. Today he told me I've got acute myelogenous leukemia." I was in absolute terror and could not believe Evan would have to go through some of the most torturous treatment known to modern medicine.

As Evan received the diagnosis in the fall of 1985, I felt like we were on the eve of war with no army, no ammo, and little hope. When Evan began treatment, he withdrew from everything familiar, including everyone in our family. Evan's girlfriend was the insulation between him and the rest of the world. Jackie Reingold spent twelve-hour days at the hospital, sometimes sleeping in his hospital bed with him. No one was allowed in the room without Jackie present. Most of the time Evan did not want visitors, even my parents and me. Jackie and Evan started a macrobiotic diet and developed a radical attitude toward the hospital doctors, allowing no test or procedure unless it was fully explained. This did not go over big at Memorial Sloan-Kettering.

After months of chemotherapy, remissions, and recurring cancer, it was determined that the last-ditch effort to save Evan's life would be a bone marrow transplant. My brother and parents ultimately relocated to Johns Hopkins in Baltimore, where doctors were having some success with transplants. Although the family members, including myself, were tested for compatibility, there was no match of bone marrow. Evan had an autologous transplant, in which his own marrow was harvested, treated, and replaced in his body. This extreme medical procedure caused much tension and anxiety, as it was Evan's final hope for life.

Whenever I visited the hospital I was noticeably upset and my Tourette symptoms were exacerbated. Most of my visits were met with scathing expressions from the staff in response to my twitching and, understandably, little patience from Evan. After his transplant, Evan was quarantined because his immune system was no more developed than a newborn's, and no one was allowed to touch him. I could not stop Tourettically tapping his ankle, however, which caused Evan to become angry at me and my Tourette syndrome, as if I were a nuisance. The nurse looked at me strangely and said, "What is the matter with you?"

"I've got a neurological disorder," I answered, but Evan exploded.

"Lowell, maybe she doesn't know what a neurological disorder is." How can a nurse in a hospital not know what a neurological disorder is? I thought.

It was only about five years between the time I was diagnosed with Tourette, and the onset of Evan's illness. In some ways I was still resolving my own problems accepting Tourette. I felt overwhelmed by sadness and desperation.

■ ■ ■

Orrin and Jill were very upset for me during that last shoot. As a doctor, therapist, and fellow Touretter, Orrin had a good idea what the next few years would hold for my family, but he also gave me hope in a time filled with crisis.

During this time Evan reflected on religion and his own death. The idea of Jesus occupied his thoughts, even though our family is Jewish and agnostic. "People say He's testing you to see how you come out of it. I don't buy that," Evan said. I told him about a train ride I had on the way to the hospital. I was twitching and jerking uncontrollably when a young woman approached me and said, "Jesus heals, you only have to believe."

"Why would He make it conditional?" Evan continued. "Why blackmail me? If He comes to me tonight I would welcome Him." Given his own closeness to death, Evan wanted to believe, and I remembered the saying, "There are no atheists in foxholes." But Evan also wanted to know that God loved him and would save him unconditionally, even if he could not himself believe unconditionally.

I visited Evan late one night when he was further along in the chemotherapy process. Thinking I had the right room number on the twelfth floor of Memorial Sloan-Kettering, I tried to approach quietly—patients were sleeping. I had bought some flowers in the lobby and was looking forward to seeing my brother, even considering these awful circumstances. I carefully peeked inside the room and noticed an embryonic-looking, beet-red man lying in a fetal position. He was bald and looked small, almost shriveled. Thinking I had the wrong room I turned to walk away when I heard Evan's familiar voice

"Lowell, it's me."

I was shocked . . . Evan was unrecognizable.

■ ■ ■

Six months later, after my brother's discharge from the hospital during a remission, he continued treatment on an outpatient basis. We began to meet at the Ackerman Institute, a family therapy center with a program specializing in helping terminally ill people. Our therapist, the director of the program, was a very tall, thin, Australian man named Dr. John Patton. He was a great negotiator of emotions without getting emotional himself. If one of us became unduly excited or if we raised our voices Dr. Patton raised his arm, as if to form a brace or put distance between the two parties.

I remember one session vividly because it involved Dr. Patton and Evan privately discussing the possibility of imminent death. Dr. Patton, with his cool, controlled manner, instructed each of us to hug and say good-bye to Evan. My father and mother were in the room with Evan, my sister, Lillian, who had made a special trip from Pennsylvania, and me. The atmosphere was still and tense, yet sorrowful. Evan was eager to hug each of us and tell us how he felt. My father was in a chair across from me, his glasses off, wiping his face with his hand and a handkerchief. My mother was next to Evan, holding his right hand and stroking his bald head. "I love you all very much," Evan cried, "and I'm sorry this had to happen." He went around the room and embraced each of us. Lillian wept quietly. We all sobbed as Evan said good-bye, and I remember feeling guilty about being healthy and making plans to travel while Evan was making plans for death.

As Evan became increasingly sick, his and my role in our family reversed. Evan wielded power over us, orchestrating not only the strategy of our family therapy but also the path of his recovery.

During therapy sessions my symptoms were visibly worse. I was a constant tornado of tics, kicking, shouting, and extending my arms into everyone's faces. It was distracting and upsetting. I loved Evan, we had lived together as roommates for years after leaving home and had many friends in common. When he told me he didn't want to spend time with me, I felt rejected not only by my brother but by my best friend as well. "It's because your Tourette is difficult to take," he told me simply.

"Maybe I shouldn't be around you because you've got cancer," I retorted defensively. I was crying uncontrollably and looked to Dr. Patton for help. I realized we had all come to depend on him for support. The doctor put one hand on Evan's shoulder and then one on mine.

"How do you feel?" he said.

"Attacked," Evan said.

Then I related a dream I had had a few nights earlier.

"It was the middle of the night, and I woke up startled. I was lying in an empty grave, face up. People were piling dirt on me with shovels—burying me alive." Evan looked intensely across the room at me, his red face tight with a mixture of anger and concern. He was crying, too. Our parents, once pillars of strength and stability in our lives, were watching closely, sadly, their spirits broken by these events. Suddenly, Mom and Dad looked like scared children, and Evan and me elderly brothers with the weight of the world on our shoulders. Dr. Patton asked us to stand and face each other.

"You are brothers. Do you love each other?" Dr. Patton asked.

Evan and I both said, "Yes." We hugged and cried. Finally I said, "Evan, it should have been me, I'm the defective one."

For a lifetime I was the son with something "wrong," to whom all attention was drawn. Now I felt healthy because I knew Evan was deathly ill, but maybe jealous because everything revolved around him. The situation of being in a weakened, disadvantaged position in a family can also be one of great power. The sick person has the potential to rule and can sometimes be a tyrant. Everyone listened to Evan and obeyed because we knew he might not be around for long. Evan became revered as an elder might be—and feared because he represented the power of death.

■ ■ ■

Through the years Evan learned, by necessity, to become his own best health advocate. He also became a master orator of his story, performing a full-length monologue off Broadway to critical acclaim. *Time on Fire* related nothing less than the story of a fight for life against all odds. My parents and sister and I learned to accommodate each other's needs. Evan's bone marrow transplant proved successful and he is considered cured. Dr. John Patton died of AIDS. I began a journey of many months' travel with Oliver Sacks. My photos of Art Bailey, originally done for *Life*, were published around the world. They were also shown as part of an exhibition celebrating two hundred years of art and science at the Grand Palais in Paris. Dr. Orrin Palmer is a successful neuropsychiatrist practicing in Frederick, Maryland. Howard Chapnick contracted amyotrophic lateral sclerosis (ALS), or Lou Gehrig's disease, and died of an unrelated illness. My family is glad to be alive and even though it has taken years of recovery, we try to look ahead to a time with less tragedy and more hope.

# 6. Jet Set Tourette

**H**ow are we driven by Tourette and all of its influences? Are we prisoners in our own bodies? Does it distort reality, diminish free will? Is it an exaggerated expression of will? Does it create a "state of being," as Oliver Sacks says, or is it just a movement disorder? Can Tourette result in a changed reality with everything formed around the "will" of the disorder and its demands?

As I began to work more closely with Oliver Sacks, I wondered why he was so fascinated by people with Tourette. Was this thing simply an aberration or, as in Oliver's mind, a universe? Were we really friends or was I simply another specimen for the doctor to observe? In 1988, Oliver Sacks, neurologist and best-selling author of *Awakenings*, and I were about to leave for what became several months of travel, research, and investigation concerning one of Oliver's favorite subjects: Tourette syndrome.

Tourette is often accompanied by a quick wit and agile intelligence that provide a coping mechanism through difficult social situations. At this time, my symptoms were fairly middle of the road. They were not as bad as some people we were to encounter but noticeable nonetheless. I am quite tactile. I like touching objects as well as people. If I touch something or someone with my left hand, I must touch with my right hand to obtain an equally satisfying feeling. I let out loud grunts followed by mouth-popping, lip-smacking sounds. At the same instant, my arm may jerk away from my body or I may stomp my foot. These disruptions last only a second or two, but the reactions I receive in public cause more discomfort than the Tourettic sensations. After Touretting I always look to see if anyone is staring. When I inevitably find they are, I stare back in defiance, only prolonging the embarrassment, bewilderment, or, worse, outrage on strangers' faces.

Oliver is a large man with a salt-and-pepper beard that wraps around his face. His shirt pocket is always filled with pens and he carries an assortment of notebooks as well as a cushion for his bad back. Many people have asked me, "Does Dr. Sacks have Tourette?" Oliver does not have

Dr. Oliver Sacks, who I would get to know extremely well during our years of travel together studying Tourette's.

Tourette except by association, and in his own halting, uneven speech, combined with sudden mannerisms, Oliver has adopted certain superficial aspects of the neurological disorder. It made his quest that much easier; the Touretters related to him.

Oliver liked calling those of us who have the disorder Touretters; in fact he invented the term, a term that some like and some hate. But he had only seen a glimpse of it. I was going to show him every impulse, every twitch. In our month-long journey we were to meet identical twins with Tourette in Phoenix and Atlanta, a cursing writer in California, a compulsive ex-anorexic in Los Angeles, and in New Orleans a Tourettic businessman obsessed with details of the television show *Star Trek*.

Oliver and I had agreed to rendezvous in West Los Angeles at the home of Muriel Seligman, whom I had gotten to know during my work with the Orphan Drug Act. Her high-rise apartment, with a view of Westwood, was where Oliver and I stayed for a week while Muriel was away. The good doctor and I were the guests of her son, Adam, a writer and music critic with severe Tourette syndrome.

"Hi, Lowell, fuck, cunt, shit, how are you?" Oliver and Adam had met before and seemed comfortable talking. I asked Adam about his swearing, and the evolution of this symptom.

"In 1980, fuck me, my coprolalia had just started up again. I didn't have it for six years. From nine to eleven, I said the word 'bullshit,' which was a wonderful word to say in public school. I said 'shit' and 'bullshit,' no other words. At seventeen it came back with the words 'fuck,' 'bullshit,' 'titties,' and the word 'cunt' started at eighteen."

Years later, Adam would give me this update. "The most recent thing with the coprolalia is that during the Rodney King trial, the word 'nigger' showed up, which was very traumatizing. My theory about all Tourette symptoms," Adam continued, "is that you have a buildup of pressure, which must be relieved by an action. The action is either a physical movement, a sound, a ritualistic compulsive act, or an obsessive thought. If you don't relieve this pressure it builds up, and you feel like you are going to explode. With me, I feel it in my diaphragm, I feel it in my neck, and I have had some minor bouts of self-injurious behavior. The worst was at fourteen, I had a mouth tic where I literally ripped a hole in my gums. I had to have surgery."

In spite of this difficult situation, Adam remained an articulate writer and a fine music critic, with a number of loyal editors who supported his work. Because he was able to write at home and not in an office, he successfully circumvented his disability.

Adam, Oliver, and I took a stroll around Westwood as we talked. At first Oliver was very shy, and I think he felt it too intrusive to ask me questions about my disorder. I wanted to pull Oliver's long salt-and-pepper beard, but I knew this would

have to wait until we knew each other better. But if Oliver often found intimate conversation on delicate subjects disturbing, he found distraction and relief in contact with vegetation. Oliver had contemplated becoming a botanist before choosing a career in medicine and suggested the walk.

"Stop, look," Oliver would say with Tourettic speed, "a cycad!" We had stopped at a residence with a beautiful lawn and some plantings. Oliver pointed to a type of gymnosperm that resembled a small palm. "It's lovely," he continued, as he knelt on one knee to put his face to the plant. Oliver smelled the cycad and plucked a small leaf from the tree. I wondered what the people who lived in this house would think if they saw a 275-pound man with a huge beard sniffing their plants.

Oliver also had a fascination for mathematics, specifically geometry. We asked a passerby directions to a specific part of town. "Do you know the way to Bel Air?" Oliver asked. The man explained in convoluted terms the way to get to our destination, which Oliver interpreted as "it's two sides of an isosceles triangle."

"Oliver, why is everything like a geometry lesson with you?" I asked. "Let's take a left here and make it a trapezoid."

"You two are like a married couple," Adam said. "Fuck me, let's go home."

Adam lived in an apartment in Santa Monica, while Oliver and I were sharing Muriel's two bedrooms. Both Muriel and Adam had been instrumental in the success of the Southern California Tourette Syndrome Association chapter, and Adam invited us to an upcoming meeting at City of Hope, a medical center in Duarte, California. Oliver had heard of Dr. David Comings and his medical center and thought the visit would be a fine idea. Oliver had wanted a finished piece of writing to come out of this experience, and he wanted me to feel as if I was part of it. We all said good night and made plans to meet the next morning.

I had a fitful night's sleep as someone might being in a new place and awoke with the realization of a bizarre dream. As we got in our car to go I said, "I had a dream that you were painting a giant canvas, and I was there watching. I can't remember a lot of it, but you had a brush and it was going to be in a museum."

"Lowell, I hope you realize that you are making the painting with me," Oliver said. "I'm not doing it alone."

"I guess so, but in the dream, you were painting."

"We must go for an emergency dream interpretation," Oliver stammered. "Get Bob Rodman on the car phone." Robert Rodman was a psychiatrist in Pacific Palisades and author of *Not Dying*, written about his wife's battle with cancer. I had become obsessed with the dream and its imagined meaning, as Touretters sometimes do.

"I wouldn't worry about it," Oliver said, after finding Bob was not home. "Just try to imagine we are both creating the painting."

After this slight diversion, we returned to West Los Angeles and find Adam, who was sitting outside Muriel's apartment with a friend.

"This is Julie, she has Tourette, too," Adam said. Julie was an attractive woman in her early twenties. She was petite with very long, light brown hair. As we both planned to attend the meeting at City of Hope, Julie and I began to talk. She was extremely thin, and I discovered she was recovering from anorexia, having gained twenty pounds in the past couple of months. She looked very good, actually, and conversing with her was comfortable and direct. We decided to go for a drive: Adam drove with Oliver next to him, and I sat in the back with Julie.

During a pause in our talk, I realized that Julie had her hand on my thigh. Her hand was not simply resting, she was tracing a figure eight on my leg. It was somewhat odd, but I didn't say anything, and she continued to draw. It's not that I minded Julie's hand on my leg, it's just that I wasn't sure if this was affection, Tourette, or something else. Later that evening, back at Muriel's, I asked Julie about the figure eights.

"It's an enclosure thing," she said. "A feeling I have when I'm drawing. It's like the edges are rough, and I'm smoothing them down. Then I draw a figure eight the other way, with a stem on it, and it's a flower. I do it all in my mind. The idea is to draw without lifting the pencil. It's a game."

The next morning we were scheduled to go to City of Hope, located in a desert area about an hour from Los Angeles. Dr. David Comings and his wife greeted us when we arrived. David was a geneticist at the medical center and a preeminent researcher on the subject of Tourette. About a hundred people were there for the meeting. Julie was a regular. Before a talk conducted by a panel of experts, Dr. Comings introduced Oliver and me, telling the crowd about our travels across the country. After the meeting, we went outside and sat in on a talk session, commonly described as a "rap group," where people discussed their problems with Tourette syndrome. David presided over this therapeutic session, where I learned Julie not only had Tourette but also OCD. This explained the figure-eight drawing as an action Julie felt necessary to complete. Perhaps like some others with OCD, she felt if she did not complete an action, bad consequences would result. I used to kick objects such as walls, tables, chairs, or doors. It's not that I wanted to, rather I found it impossible to stop. I tested just how hard I could kick without breaking something. Sometimes my foot went through the wall in my apartment. I empathized with Julie and realized I had some of the same irresistible urges.

After Julie spoke, I began to notice David Comings. He was a fairly tall man in his fifties with white hair and an inquisitive expression. David's interest in and dedication to those with Tourette was, and still is, great. His wife wore tall boots, the kind they had in the sixties, and I imagined her to be fairly bored by the rap session. I couldn't help but observe a self-absorbed atmosphere at City of Hope, with Dr. Comings as scientific guru. These people were almost like his disciples, but was it really that different from any other organization or group, with a leader and people who have a common interest or belief? Perhaps each school, medical center, or office building has its own gurus and followers.

Once the meeting let out, Julie and I began to make eyes at each other. She was cute and friendly, and we both knew we were interested in each other. Back in Adam's car, Julie resumed her figure eights. I had always wondered what it might be like to make love with a woman who, like me, has

Tourette. During sex and sleep are the only times a Touretter does not twitch and that seems to up the sexual ante. By the time Adam dropped us off at Muriel's apartment we were all over each other. Oliver was eager to do a formal interview with Julie, and I was anxious for something else. The three of us were left to discuss the subject that brought us together.

"I can control it, there is a control thing," Julie said referring to her compulsive petting. "I know with whom I can get away with it and when I can't." Oliver was intrigued and questioned Julie further. I let them talk for a long time but as night fell I was getting restless. I also knew Julie wanted to be rescued from the doctor's probing questions. I had gone into the bedroom to watch television and when I emerged it was to bring Julie back with me.

"It's getting late, Oliver," I said, and Julie got the hint.

"Yeah, I'm tired," Julie said. "Maybe that's enough for tonight." We went into my bedroom and did not come out until morning.

The next day, after Julie left, Oliver said, "You hustled me, I don't like that." He was angry that I hurried his session with Julie. But Dr. Sacks was also upset that I compromised his position as scientist by my intimacy with Julie. I did not feel the same allegiance to this code of behavior and as often happens, I let my emotions rule. Oliver and I generally got along wonderfully, but there was also a slight tension in our relationship. I think it had less to do with personality than our sometimes conflicting roles in this mission. Oliver is a scientist and a writer, and I am a photographer, but I also had an agenda of exploration and discovery and sought answers to my basic human questions about this disorder such as why must I engage in actions I do not want to do. Why do I shout and jerk my way down the street? This was just as much a mystery to me, even though I have the disorder. And so I learned something from my night with Julie. Having sex with a Touretter is not particularly different from having sex with a non-Touretter. The commonalty that we share with the Tourette is perhaps a heightened sexuality, but there is also a commonalty of humankind. We all have similar desires, pleasures, disappointments, and hopes. I liked Julie just because I liked her.

■ ■ ■

On a spectacularly sunny late February afternoon Oliver decided to take me to the house he lived in more than twenty years earlier as a resident in neurology at the University of California. Topanga Canyon is a picturesque valley a short distance from the city of Los Angeles with lush vegetation everywhere. The botanist in Oliver was excited as he shouted, "Nasturtium! Pull over to the side of the road, Lowell!" I got us off the road, and Oliver began admiring what looked to me like a weed growing out of the gravel. Oliver explained that this is a very edible herb, a kind of lettuce. "Mmm, beautiful nasturtium," Oliver said as he grazed, stooped over with the car door open. I sampled some and found it was really quite delicious. Driving through the base of the canyon we stopped for lunch. While talking over cold beer and sandwiches, Oliver told me his years here were not all happy. He was plagued by excesses in his life and was a loner. Oliver rode a huge motorcycle in those days and lifted weights at Muscle Beach. One spring day in the clinic he invited a young woman who had lost use of her legs for a ride on his bike and a picnic. It was irregular and raised eyebrows at the university, but it was Oliver at his best—compassionate and involved. Now in his late fifties, Oliver was a great success but still wondered if he had lost touch with his earlier, involved self. Was he now more of a spectator than a participant in the events around him?

We finished our lunch and continued into the higher

switchback roads that defined this canyon. Oliver's old house was a modest but wonderfully situated, split-level at the end of a short street. As we looked at the house, Oliver said, "I fear that life is passing me by and has been doing so for twenty years." Oliver was in one of his mood swings, feeling alternately elated and removed. I thought it odd that such an articulate, successful man would feel this way but was moved by Oliver's confiding in me. I too often play the observer's role rather than being a participant myself. Oliver's mannerisms, particularly his unsure, halting speech or his sudden jumping up to examine some plant, was what made him appear Tourettic. I think Oliver felt an affinity with us Touretters. Many people have commented that there is a universal desire to be provocative or disrupt the status quo. Even the shyest individuals wish they could be less inhibited. Those of us with Tourette cannot help letting loose in the most inappropriate situations. I remember a friend once said, "Lowell, it's like everybody has Tourette. I have urges to curse or kick. We all have these urges."

It was time for Oliver and me to leave the canyon and, in fact, to leave California. We were scheduled to drive to Phoenix where we would talk to others dealing with Tourette.

■ ■ ■

We drove through Nevada and into northern Arizona, which was extraordinary with the high desert on the verge of blooming. The next day we drove to Scottsdale in time for a meeting at the home of members of the Arizona chapter of the Tourette Syndrome Association. Many people attended and we talked in one large group for a period of time.

Among those gathered was a pair of identical twin boys, eleven years old and both with Tourette. Oliver was especially fascinated by the idea of identical twins with the disorder. There is a strong genetic component in Tourette and it often occurs in families. We met numerous brothers and sisters with the disorder, but twins were special.

Jared and Joel were tall boys with short, light brown hair and pleasing smiles. Their parents, Kathy and Wayne Anderson, allowed us to talk to the twins privately. Jared and Joel had mild cases of Tourette, a state of being I have come to think of as simply a "difference" rather than a deficiency. At times the twins seemed to simply have an excess of energy. "I'm supercharged for action," a Touretter from Toronto had once explained to me. Jared and Joel didn't have any such extravagant ideas, and I knew they didn't think of themselves as disabled either. Joel let out a screeching sound, not ear piercing but high-pitched, which lasted just a moment. Both boys made a lot of hand gestures and what seemed to be body expressions. Joel contorted his body at the waist with a twisting motion, but

The twins Jared and Joel Anderson often syncopated their movements.

just for a second, and then relaxed.

As we talked, the twins explained that their biggest problem was in school, taking timed tests. About 50 percent of all people with Tourette syndrome have some form of learning disability, especially attention deficit disorder. ADD, as it is commonly called, involves an inability to concentrate and focus on one subject due to a neurological problem. In Tourette syndrome, independent of learning disabilities, the motor tics (or repetitive involuntary movements) alone can cause a disruption in a student's ability to concentrate. This is why in many schools students with learning disabilities like dyslexia, which is also neurological, are allowed to take untimed tests. But even with occasional teasing from classmates, Joel and Jared enjoyed their school days and social interactions, thanks to understanding teachers and friends, and caring parents.

Watching the twins play with one of their friends, I could see that both twins were very animated, but was this animation due to an organic disorder or simply the enthusiasm of eleven-year-old boys? The twins had cleverly integrated their exuberance into their personalities. Broad strokes of an arm guiding a toy plane in for a landing seemed appropriate. Even the neck twisting and head turning they both frequently displayed, when masqueraded by outlandish play, could appear "normal." Many Touretters integrate aspects of their disorder into everyday life, masking or making use of movements that might otherwise stand out as "strange." In my own experience, I often incorporate odd movements into seemingly more acceptable gestures. In this way Touretters' actions become part of who we are.

Both boys agreed it was comforting to have an identical twin brother with Tourette. "If it was just me I'd be embarrassed," Jared said, "but with a twin it's pretty good."

"It's nice to have a twin," Joel agrees, "because you're not the only person who has it. You don't feel alone." On an ironic note he added, "It keeps us energetic."

■ ■ ■

After a couple of days touring the historic points of Tucson, the high point being a lizard skin factory, Oliver and I caught our flight to New Orleans and arrived a few nights after Mardi Gras, as the city was just recovering. Taking a taxi to the French Quarter we checked in at the Cornstalk Fence Hotel. I stood for a moment and tried to remember my time here on Royal Street, directly across from where Trios Restaurant was ten years earlier. I thought about the night at the Heads Inn and what different circumstances I am in today.

The air smelled like beer and Creole food. Crowds were out until late at night listening to jazz and drinking. It seemed the hotel did not have two rooms, so Oliver and I shared one. We arranged our respective sleeping areas and settled in for the night. At least there were two beds in the room.

Until this time, we stayed in separate rooms so I didn't

realize just how difficult it was for Oliver to fall asleep. He often read for hours before falling off into his dream state. But he explained to me that before getting into bed he had to have everything perfectly ready for sleep so he wouldn't awake during the night. Pillows would have to be propped up, and the light had to be left on all night because if he were to reach to turn it off, he'd never be able to fall asleep again. He got completely ready for bed, including regulating the room temperature to between forty-five and fifty degrees. With the window open and the light next to his bed on, we began to talk. I mentioned my night with Julie and the type of woman I'd like to meet in New Orleans. Oliver said he'd like to bring home four or five people, possibly some animals, perhaps some plant life. He liked to exaggerate his appetite for companionship. We talked more intimately than usual that night, about each other, and Tourette. We also talked about what our New Orleans host Cliff, a Tourettic businessman we had contacted through the association, might be like.

The next morning we met Cliff for breakfast. He was a short, serious man who was eager to help us on our quest. Cliff was one of those people who you thought might take themselves, and everything else, too seriously. He talked about Tourette in very scientific rather than experiential terms, about medication and symptoms. The odd thing about it was that Cliff showed no signs of having the disorder, something he attributed to self-control and medication. I thought in some way Cliff really hated Tourette, as a pest or intruder. Oliver grew tired of Cliff quickly, until we decided to take a tour of New Orleans in Cliff's car. Cliff was comfortable driving, and as we crossed Canal Street, leaving the French Quarter and heading up St. Charles Avenue, he began an astounding story.

"I was in the service working in the missile silos," Cliff explained. "You know, the missiles to start World War Three. During the four years I was in the service the order to start the missiles was almost given on three separate occasions. I had dreams at night that I turned the key to start the war. It was awful. Finally I was discharged, and the doctor claimed I was psychotic because of my Tourette."

Oliver and I were amazed but we both remained quiet. Oliver was sitting next to Cliff up front, and I was in the back just behind the driver's seat. His story was incredible, historically as well as pathologically. I think the story upset me because I immediately had a violent Tourettic convulsion, slamming into Cliff's seat and grunting loudly. "I know you have Tourette syndrome, Lowell," Cliff responded, "but you are going to have to try to control yourself." Kicking the back of seats in planes or cars was not an unusual Tourettic urge. Why did Cliff have such little tolerance for someone who suffers from the same problem?

As if our experience with Cliff hadn't been strange enough, in parting he gave us some final instruction. "One last thing," Cliff said, standing next to the driver's side of his car. "When you tell my story, please refer to me as 'Spock.'" With that, he flipped the sun visor on the driver's side down, revealing a carefully constructed picture of the *Star Ship Enterprise*, the futuristic spaceship portrayed in television's *Star Trek*, and I wondered if he was then heading off for some interplanetary adventure.

■ ■ ■

After a week in New Orleans, Oliver and I again rented a car and drove north to Atlanta. There we were to meet another pair of Tourettic identical twins, two women in their midtwenties. On the drive through Mississippi and Georgia I occasionally photographed scenes that attracted me. Oliver was pleased to stop for a few minutes when I saw something interesting, like an old woman hanging wash out to dry or a sign announcing wood for sale. He supported creative urges as well as neurological ones, I supposed.

The Atlanta twins, Carla and Claudia, were
constantly in motion. Photo by Oliver Sacks.

Once in Atlanta,
we were struck by what a modern, bustling urban center it
was. The city seemed much bigger than I had imagined.
We checked into a small motel and in the morning drove
to the suburban area where Carla and Claudia Huntey still
lived with their parents, Sylvia and Robert. As their mother

opened the door, we were greeted by a barrage of background banter from Carla and Claudia.

"Dr. Swami and Lowell Handler," Carla said, inventing her own name for Oliver.

"Lowell Handler and Dr. Swami," Claudia said. Then, without warning, she screamed loudly, "Get it out forever, get it out forever!" Both twins had a severe jumping tic, whereby they alternately jumped two feet into the air, crashing down a second later. This resulted in a constant rumbling because when one twin was in the air, the other was getting ready to jump. When the other was airborne, the first one crashed to the floor. And so it went, throughout the visit. Sylvia was eager to explain what it was like when the twins were younger.

"They were diagnosed when they were fifteen years old. We thought they were just hyper," she explained. "We took them to psychiatrists, psychologists, different doctors. They all said, 'Oh, they'll grow out of it.' I had never heard of Tourette before, ever. We were astounded that such a thing could be. One bad enough, but double?"

Carla and Claudia were both very attractive, but their voices were hoarse and raspy from screaming. They had both finished high school but were unable to find employment because of the disorder, or, more accurately, people's reaction to it. I asked the twins about the sentences they were repeating. They said that "get it out forever" was about Tourette. They wanted to get it out forever.

There was another aspect to the twins that was interesting. They constantly touched each other. When Carla touched Claudia, just a tap on the arm or leg, Claudia returned the tap. This would go on indefinitely until interrupted by jumping or screaming. When I touch objects or people I think of it as a grounding mechanism, like a lightning rod. I somehow feel better, or more secure, after I have touched something. Carla said there were some things she could explain, like the inability to inhibit her actions and others she couldn't, like the touching. During the few hours at the twins' house, there was a lot of talking, screeching, and running around, but I don't know if we came up with any real answers. Not that we were supposed to. The whole trip was an exploration, a slow, sometimes painful process of discovery.

■ ■ ■

As I sat beside Oliver on the flight home to New York, I fantasized about a day when Tourette wouldn't exist anymore. Tourette raises questions that could shed light on many aspects of human nature: perception, humor, ego, the nature of difference, and camaraderie among those who are different. I never realized the incredible scope and range of people who have this thing, people with the same urges, motivations, and etiologies. As I watched Oliver sleep, I finally realized we are all different, no two of us the same, not even the twins. Those of us who have Tourette all have it differently. But though we are different, there is something that binds those of us with this disorder. Perhaps it's shared experiences or an understanding of motivations. Oliver, as our unofficial mascot, understands us.

When we landed in New York, it was time for Oliver and me to go our separate ways, even though we shared a great deal during the past few weeks. At the baggage claim it occurred to me I would miss Oliver and the Touretters we visited. The experience had helped me realize I wasn't alone. People everywhere have Tourette; it's not as rare as we think.

Just then, Oliver looked at me and said, "It's been a good trip, Lowell." I knew he was right. Our journey had given me a wider perspective, a somewhat more open-minded way of viewing the world.

# 7. Pot and Prozac Love

**E**ver since my discovery of Tourette, I'd searched for relief from my symptoms, which seemed to come and go with a will of their own. Now, in my apartment in Cold Spring, New York, I slowly, and then with alarming frequency, experienced repeated outbreaks of obsessive-compulsive traits. Like others with Tourette, I had obsessive thoughts, intrusive recurring notions that were difficult to control. The compulsions would be seen in physical actions that had no apparent purpose, yet it seemed necessary to complete the action to obtain tactile or mental satisfaction.

Many people with Tourette have obsessive-compulsive aspects of their personalities, without having full-blown

OCD. I had always had some of these symptoms, but they had never been exhibited with such force. When I finished a drink, I would tap the glass on the counter in order to feel the base against the Formica. As if testing the limits of the materials, as well as my own patience and vulnerability, I'd continue tapping until I slammed the glass against the counter, the kitchen table, or another glass, ultimately breaking objects one by one. This pattern continued for months until every glass and dish in my apartment was smashed.

Research has suggested that people with Tourette syndrome have low frustration thresholds, and when I was upset or angry my own symptoms became exacerbated. During one of Evan's stays in the hospital, I arrived home one afternoon after a visit during which he had been unwilling or unable to talk to me. My work wasn't going well at the time. I was broke and exasperated and took my frustration out on yet another set of glasses. As I gazed at the shattered glass, I thought about Evan lying in the hospital and felt a storm of rage inside me. I also felt guilty, again, that I was healthy and Evan was on what we thought was his deathbed. Looking at the evidence of my anger made me more enraged, but I avoided cleaning up the mess for hours, fearing I might do it again.

Instead, I began to pound the walls of my apartment and finally smashed my size-thirteen shoe completely through the Sheetrock. I continued to kick large holes through the walls during the next few hours, feeling a release of energy each time, and through this outburst, temporary relief. My violence was never directed at others, but in this case I saw this expression of violence as a self-inflicted punishment for escaping the cancer that caught Evan and the rest of our family by surprise.

As my compulsive symptoms worsened, *Newsweek* ran a cover story touting Prozac as a new miracle drug. I had heard people's stories of rejuvenation and revival with Prozac. Orrin Palmer, the doctor with Tourette syndrome I had photographed for *Life* told me, "It revolutionized my life." A woman I met in a bar said, "I would not be alive today if it weren't for Prozac."

Prozac (fluoxetine hydrochloride) was approved by the FDA in the late eighties and represented the newest class in a series of drugs that had been used to treat depression. From Dr. Palmer I learned more about the three most commonly used types of antidepressants: monoamine oxidase (MAO) inhibitors, tricyclics, and selective serotonin reuptake inhibitors (SSRI), including Prozac. All of these

drugs worked by affecting different chemical neurotransmitters in the brain. Like a complex system of electrical cir-
cuits, the brain is wired with millions of receptor cells, each
designed to receive the message of a particular chemical
neurotransmitter. The message is sent across a synapse, or
juncture, where the impulse passes from one neuron to
another. Before Prozac, the most commonly used anti-
depressant was the tricyclic, named for its three-ring molecu-
lar structure. While many patients reported improvements
in their mood, because the drug affected a number of neurotransmitters, some patients were bothered by excessive side
effects such as dry mouth, constipation, blurred vision, mild
short-term memory loss, and weight gain.

In 1980, a team of doctors began work on a new genera-
tion of antidepressants that would concentrate on a single
neurotransmitter, serotonin, believed to be significantly responsible for depression as well as OCD. Serotonin, which
is released throughout the brain, affects many kinds of behavior, including mood regulation, stress tolerance, and the
ability to inhibit impulses. Messages come from the higher
centers of the brain, such as the neocortex, to the basal
ganglia, which coordinates motor function, where they are
processed. SSRIs block the absorption of serotonin by the

receptors, thus creating an excess of serotonin in the synapse area. Scientists extrapolate that this increased level of serotonin corrects an imbalance or defect in the brain's own ability to produce or transmit serotonin along the chemical pathways. Because SSRIs act specifically on serotonin, and not a wide range of neurotransmitters, they have less annoying side effects.

There are at least twelve different serotonin receptors in the brain, each one having a different capacity to bind with the chemical. Some regulate mood, which affects depression, while others inhibit intrusive thoughts or actions, which affects obsessive-compulsive symptoms. Fluoxetine hydrochloride was approved by the FDA in the late eighties but was not widely popular until 1990, and was approved specifically for OCD a couple of years after that. Different doses of Prozac are used to control OCD, an anxiety disorder, and depression.

I spoke with Dr. David Dunner, a professor and vice chairman in the Department of Psychiatry and Behavioral Sciences at the University of Washington in Seattle and a pioneer in this area, about the arrival of this groundbreaking drug. Dunner was one of the researchers investigating fluoxetine in clinical trials for almost a decade before Prozac came on the market. "What we have done in the past twenty years," he argues, "is develop a database about treatment outcome that is very good for choosing what treatment works. Secondly, we have developed rather specific treatments and have shown they are effective, and those treatments encompass both psychotherapy and medication."

I then asked how he looked philosophically at the question of treating a patient with a pill rather than therapy. This idea that we have created a "quick fix" to complex problems has been the subject of debate in our society for years. "I think the notion of these disorders being psychological is probably wrong," he responded. "What we've learned about a number of conditions is that in many instances they are inherited, familial, and possibly biological. Philosophically, I think it's terrific."

Although there had been much controversy surrounding Prozac, I felt I needed to do something about my escalating symptoms. I called my doctor, Ruth Bruun, a psychiatrist in New York City who specialized in movement disorders, and asked for a prescription. It takes at least a couple of weeks after starting the medication to feel results, and I waited patiently, somewhat apprehensively, for side effects and therapeutic benefits. I was incredibly pleased to discover no side effects, but rather tremendous relief from my obsessive-compulsive behavior. Prozac did not "cure" the obsessive-compulsive symptoms, but they were greatly diminished.

Up to this point, I had become quite reliant on marijuana for its tranquilizing effects. Before going out of the house—to a movie or on a train—I would smoke a joint, lessening my symptoms and giving me a sense of inebriation and well-being. Often I'd smoke with friends in my small town, numerous times a day, every day, and this stoned state continued even after I started with Prozac.

One of the most common and early side effects of Prozac is a restless feeling, as if one must move around and cannot sit still. This usually goes away within a few weeks of taking the medication; however, I found pot smoking counteracted this side effect right away. The feeling of euphoria—the "high" that pot is known for—is accentuated by Prozac, and I was perpetually flying. This combination of pot and Prozac became a potent way of life for me, and as the months passed I vaguely wondered if my marijuana smoking had become an addiction.

One of the people whose house was a virtual den of smoking and carrying on was Terry, a man who at that time lived down the road from my apartment in Cold Spring. Terry was in his late thirties and disabled from a serious car accident some years earlier. He had long hair in a ponytail, an earring, and he wore sandals and T-shirts. Terry smoked pot, and a lot of it, as a means of recreation, self-medication for pain, and, I imagine, habit. Terry once told me he smoked about five joints a day: one with coffee in the morning, one after lunch, one late in the afternoon, another after dinner, and a last joint at night.

There were always people coming and going at Terry's house, smoking, playing croquet, having water-gun fights as well as barbecues in the summer. There were variations and condiments to the marijuana menu. Beer, and often champagne, were stored in the refrigerator. On occasion the scene became particularly decadent when hashish was mixed with pot or brownies.

One such evening a young woman named Polly joined Terry and me. Polly was a real party girl, and I liked her casually stoned attitude. She had beautiful hair, full pink lips, and wanted to smoke and drink with us. She had helped Terry make a batch of wonderful fudge brownies from scratch and we sat around joking and eating hash brownies.

I took a long, hard drag on a joint and inhaled a mixture of glorious smoke and aroma into my lungs. As I slowly released the weed, I felt a buoyancy rise from my stomach to my head. I had already eaten a couple of brownies and was very stoned, dizzy in fact. I sat back in my chair as Terry's and Polly's chatter became superfluous. I was high as a kite and loving it, while the room around me became a spin of smoke and light air.

．．．

Pot can make you philosophical, and in my stoned and sometimes bored state I did a lot of thinking. I wondered if there was a larger meaning to having Tourette, how others had come to terms with the disorder, and particularly those who had had Tourette before anyone knew what it was.

I recalled Dr. Arthur Shapiro, who first treated me for Tourette syndrome, saying that if he had the disorder and someone asked him about it, he would respond by pointing out, "I have the same thing Samuel Johnson had." At the time, I did not know much about Dr. Johnson, who was born in 1709, wrote the first English language dictionary, and was one of the most quoted intellectuals in history. It is very interesting that many experts strongly believe Johnson had Tourette syndrome as well as obsessive-compulsive symptoms, if not the full-blown disorder.

Johnson's mother was forty years old when she gave birth to him. He described the hard birth, attempting to come to grips with the anxiety experienced during adulthood: "My mother had a very difficult and dangerous labour, and was assisted by George Hector, a man-midwife of great reputation. I was born almost dead, and could not cry for some time. I was taken home, a poor, diseased infant, almost blind."

Samuel Johnson's aunt, Mrs. Nathaniel Ford, told him years later she "would not have picked such a poor creature up in the street." At the age of twenty, Johnson had what has been described as a mental breakdown, although it has never been clearly detailed. This was more than one hundred years before Georges Gilles de la Tourette first described the syndrome that bears his name.

There have been many biographies of Johnson written over the last two hundred years. It is amazing that none of these books mentions Tourette syndrome by name, although some mention Johnson's bizarre ritualistic behavior, as well as his many tics.

One such book, Walter Jackson Bate's Pulitzer Prize-winning biography, *Samuel Johnson*, includes wonderful descriptions of Johnson's antics: "For he now began to develop the embarrassing tics and other compulsive mannerisms that were to haunt him all his life—the sort of thing that led the artist William Hogarth to say that when he first saw Johnson (at the home of Samuel Richardson, standing by a window, 'shaking his head and rolling himself about in a strange ridiculous manner'), he concluded Johnson 'was an ideot, whom his relations had put under the care of Mr. Richardson.' Then, to Hogarth's surprise, this figure stalked over to where Richardson and he were sitting, and 'all at once took up the argument, and displayed such a power of eloquence, that Hogarth looked at him with astonishment, and actually imagined that this ideot had been at the moment inspired.' "

Jack Bate, as this scholar is known to his colleagues at Harvard University, continues: "These tics and compulsive movements—often extreme—were certainly of psycho-neurotic origin and not, as has sometimes been assumed, of organic origin. They almost as certainly date from this period and not at all from early childhood, however 'awkward' or 'strange' he might sometimes have seemed to others in his earlier years."

In speaking with Bate, I stated my belief that Samuel Johnson's manifestations were the result of Tourette syndrome, which is an organic neurological disorder. "I think you are probably right," he told me. "A number of people have raised this point since the book was published."

It is also interesting that throughout Bate's book, as well as virtually all the other biographies, Johnson is described as faulting himself with a lack of control in negotiating his tics and obsessions. Consider this passage from later in *Samuel Johnson*: "And as he struggled alone against the self-conflicts, the paralysis, the inner resistance, he once again—as in his twenties—found himself also having to battle with the swarm of psychological by-products that rose up from 'self-management.' They could become so compulsive and yet be so trivial that he could feel that their tyranny over him was itself a form of 'madness.' "

In Johnson's own diaries from 1759 we see the famous author chastise himself: "Enable me to break the chain of my sins . . . and to overcome and suppress vain scruples." He later wrote: "God help me . . . to combat scruples." He constantly mentioned "scruples" in his diaries, which Bate describes as referring to his compulsive acts, from the Latin *scrupulus*, meaning a small sharp pebble.

The most remarkable aspect of Bate's beautifully written biography is that in discussing Johnson as man, moralist, and philosopher, we see a personality molded and influenced by Tourette, unbeknownst to neither the author nor, of course, his subject.

In the following passage, Bate places Johnson's philosophy in historical context, and perhaps in pathological context as well:

"As in no other classical moralist, we have a profound anticipation of what was to be the wide-scale nineteenth and twentieth century discovery about the mind that went on from the major Romantics down through the clinical exploration of the unconscious that follows Freud. That is, the discovery that the mind—far from being either a serene, objective, rational instrument, or, as the radical materialist thought, a sort of recording machine that works in mechanically happy union with whatever outside experiences press the button—is something unpredictably alive in its own right. And when something outside stimulates or pokes it into activity, it can start moving in any number of unforeseen ways that are by no means in harmony with things outside it."

Bate has uncovered here what is precisely the essence of Tourette—that the mind has a mind of its own. Like Tourette, life is unpredictable and erratic.

We define an individual's life, to a large extent, within the context of the time in which that life occurred. After Johnson's time, during the Romantic period, the idea of a glorified and idealized humanity prevailed. Freudian categorization, which arrived later, showed man to be flawed and ruled by passion. In between, we were to experience a golden age of neurology, which Johnson did not live to see, but which would explain Tourette syndrome as a physiological phenomenon much as we view it today.

It has been assumed for hundreds of years that Johnson's obsessive, compulsive, and tic-rich behavior was the result of a mental breakdown possibly due to physical illness at birth. We can now theorize, with some evidence, that Samuel Johnson did have Tourette syndrome and through the lens of his affliction he was able to illuminate the nature of thought in an unprecedented manner.

Today we have a proliferation of medications available, and in my particular way I had tried to take advantage of them, often seeking relief in my own self-prescribed regimen of pot and Prozac. Johnson was without the advantage of modern pharmacology and had to face his difficulties head-on, finding consolation not in chemistry but in philosophy. "The eye is not satisfied with seeing, nor the ear filled with hearing," he wrote about his mental state more than two hundred years ago. "The natural flights of the human mind are not from pleasure to pleasure, but from hope to hope."

# 8. Susanna and Marriage

**L**ying in bed, our two naked bodies touched gently after hours of lovemaking. I leaned over and put my arms around her slim, soft waist, nibbled on the curve of her neck, and kissed her ear. We were exhausted and it was the middle of the night. We spent what seemed like endless joyful hours talking and making love. She is charming, caring, cute, and lovable, I thought. I hugged and caressed her often, thinking she enjoyed the attention. I felt so good around her, we glowed in each other's company. We could not stop talking and kissing, sharing our thoughts together. I envisioned the ensuing months with her, constantly, incessantly enveloped in her breasts.

Susanna Burgett and I were falling in love, spending our first weekend together in Newburyport, Massachusetts, after driving up the north shore from Boston. We hadn't eaten all day and the only place open was a Chinese restaurant a half mile down the road. As we walked, Susanna said, "I'm glad you showed this to me." She was referring to the *Life* magazine article I had done with Oliver. She seemed to be accepting of Tourette in a way few people were and this, along with her intelligence and good looks, drew me close to her.

Susanna and I were an unlikely pair: me a Jewish, Touretting photojournalist high on pot and Prozac, and Susanna a demure Protestant lawyer. Susanna was a petite, pretty vegetarian who grew up in Woodstock, New York. She was strong and certain in business dealings, yet restrained and tentative in relationships. I had met Susanna when she was the girlfriend of my friend Dan Price from high school. When I spoke to Dan and told him I was going to Boston for the weekend he suggested I have dinner with Susanna, who now lived there. Dan had since married and had two children. Why, I wondered, would I want to see a woman whom I last met eight years earlier. Little did I know Susanna had asked Dan about me and remembered me as "intelligent and cute." At a Chinese restaurant in Cambridge, near Susanna's apartment, we met for dinner.

Susanna worked twelve to fifteen hours a day in business law. She wanted to do other things with her time and hoped someday to have a family. On that first date, it seemed Susanna was open to beginning a relationship, and I was too. I thought she sounded very intelligent yet lonely, working constantly and spending what little free time she had at home.

In the spring of 1990 we started long-distance dating, and seeing each other whenever I was in Boston or when Susanna was visiting her family in Woodstock. As our relationship progressed, I eventually met them too. I will never forget the first weekend I was introduced to Susanna's parents. What an odd couple, I thought. Bob, her father, was a World War II veteran, a bomber pilot and sufferer of post-traumatic stress disorder (which at one time was commonly referred to as "shell shock"). After we shook hands, I noticed a battery of rifles in the corner. Bob looked at me and said, "You like guns? I've got a lot of them." Then he picked up a rifle and pointed it right at my head. I was startled and heard him say, "I don't use 'em, I just collect 'em." Bob showed me his old uniform in a bedroom closet (I noticed her parents had separate rooms), but admitted it didn't fit anymore. The whole house was filled with rickety, broken, fragile-looking antiques, and the contents rattled when I Tourettically walked on the hardwood floors. There was an incredibly musty odor, as if it were a summerhouse that hadn't been occupied in years. There were books everywhere and a thick layer of dust.

Bob went into the kitchen, where he lay down on a small cot and began to talk. I didn't really understand what he was saying, but it involved Social Security and building codes. He rambled on in a kind of monologue to no one in particular over our conversation with Susanna's mother in the living room.

Bob's banter formed the background noise for the rest of the afternoon, until he drifted off to sleep. Most of what he said seemed like nonsense, and it was almost as if he didn't expect anyone to listen. I felt bad but didn't really know what to say, and realized this scenario had been played out many times before.

Susanna's mother, Suzanne, was an intelligent, quiet woman who read a great deal and loved gardening. She had wispy white hair and pointed features.

"Thank God he's asleep. He goes on and on sometimes," she said. "Tell me about your family, Lowell." Suzanne seemed very civilized compared to Bob and wanted to hear about my parents, brother, and sister. We talked and eventually Suzanne went out to the garden. Susanna and I held hands tightly and sat on the couch.

Susanna was empathetic toward Touretters and able to see past an aberration into the person. I felt she had a unique understanding of difference because of her father. Even when I compulsively and Tourettically would squeeze her ticklish feet, she would smile and try to understand. Susanna's calm demeanor had a calming effect on me. If we went out and I was Touretting really wildly, Susanna would lean over and kiss me. When people saw someone loved me, they thought of me as more human, rather than some madman.

We began spending weekends at my apartment in Cold Spring, and our feelings for each other deepened. Time together became more than an attraction of opposites. Susanna and I fell in love with a mutual respect and commitment to each other, in spite of our differences. After long-distance dating for a year, we decided Susanna would move into my apartment. She said she would feel better about moving if we were to become engaged. With some hesitancy I agreed, and on an excursion to the town of Rhinebeck we stopped in at a store specializing in custom, handmade jewelry. We spotted a beautiful diamond ring set in gold, and we bought it. Outside I asked Susanna to marry me as we kissed and hugged and were both very happy. She secured a new job in Westchester County and we began to make plans.

It was a gorgeous spring day when, one year after our engagement, we were married, with friends and family on both sides arriving all morning. Evan was my best man. He was feeling well, three years after his bone marrow transplant. Of course Lillian and my parents were there, and all of Susanna's family, including her eighty-five-year-old grandmother. The ceremony was performed by a humanist leader who, in colorful style, incorporated many philosophies and religions into the service. To make everyone feel at ease he conducted an even-handed, neutral, and non-denominational service.

After the ceremony we adjourned to a lavish restaurant in nearby Garrison, where the staff had prepared a party in an old mansion with hors d'oeuvres, a buffet, and champagne. As evening fell, the staff opened all the doors lining the side of the building, revealing a full view of the golf course. Soft candlelight illuminated the room and a wonderful, festive atmosphere prevailed. As I visited from table to table with old friends, some I had known since child-hood, I thought, What a terrific night, a time filled with the expectation and promise of companionship and love.

Everyone danced at our wedding to a jazz band, as swing tunes played deep into the night, champagne flowed, and people who hadn't seen each other in years became reac-quainted. Oliver Sacks danced with my mother, and Su-sanna's grandmother got her favorite drink—a chocolate milk shake.

We spent our first night as husband and wife above the Plumbush restaurant in a luxuriously rustic room with a bottle of champagne, many gifts, and a bright future.

As time passed, we developed a routine of daily life. Su-sanna enjoyed the challenge of her new job and I was busy with my own photography projects. I felt fortunate to have a partner who understood my problem so well and was able to see me as an individual with a disorder rather than just a disorder without a person behind it.

But my excessive pot and Prozac cocktails, resulting in continual giddy laughter, began to annoy Susanna, and I ignored her requests to curb my drug activity. My pot smoking escalated to numerous times a day, and I became careless in my dealings with people in business and socially.

To make ends meet, my perpetually stoned neighbor

Terry took on a boarder at his house. The tenant turned out to be a cop who witnessed all the dope smoking and eventually returned bringing other police with drawn pistols. A number of people, including Terry, were busted and went through a period of probation. In spite of this, I continued to visit. Pot smoking had become an integral aspect of my behavior, which Susanna desperately wanted me to stop. When she brought this up I'd tell her, "Pot makes me feel good. I'll stop eventually, just not now."

Another thing Susanna didn't particularly enjoy during our marriage was my haphazard and seemingly uncaring ways. I often stayed out late at night during the week and became intoxicated with friends and neighbors like Terry. Susanna felt I wasn't thoughtful enough with people and found my flippant speaking manner, which I often used to disguise the jolts and repetitions of my speech, frivolous. I didn't want to be uncaring, but I was just impulsive and spontaneous. These were aspects of my character to which I thought Susanna was attracted.

There were aspects of Susanna's personality I didn't like either, such as her stiffness with people and a repression of emotion and sexuality. It was as if Susanna could not let herself go, or even begin to realize her potential because of her inhibitions. At times Susanna just seemed uptight, unable to interact with friends, or even with me. Some of this I attributed to an upbringing in which affection was rarely displayed. And Susanna always felt she had to be in control. I think her greatest fear was that she would somehow lose her precise ability to compartmentalize her actions and emotions. It was this fear, or fear of fear, that gripped Susanna for years and kept her from realizing a less inhibited life. In some sense, I felt Susanna looked to me for a window into an uninhibited, less structured, spur-of-the-moment attitude. She valued these qualities in me, as well as my ability to mingle with diverse people and ad-lib in any situation. Ironically, the same qualities Susanna admired were also those which ultimately contributed to our breaking apart.

One night, after feeling unable to talk with Susanna, I went out to a bar I frequented, owned by a friend. Sitting at the Riverview bar I struck up a conversation with a Rastafarian man from Kenya. David was visiting the United States for a few months from Nairobi and was in Cold Spring for just a few nights. As we stayed up late drinking and talking, David seemed astounded by my Tourette.

"I have never heard of such a thing," he said. "You touch

the floor, other people, objects. If I were you I'd tie my arms behind my back when I awake in the morning."

I attempted to explain to David something about brain chemistry and the impulses for my actions, but it was to no avail. David was so stuck on the thought that this was a shameful behavior, best to be hidden, that he couldn't see anything else.

He wanted to know more about my mental state, and some of his questions were insightful. "What are your dreams like?" he asked. I explained that most of my dreams consisted of the same grainy black-and-white imagery that is characteristic of my photography and were never in color. In my dreams I don't have Tourette and I don't move with the same jerky gait I have in real life. Some nights I imagine myself flying over a shoreline with waves breaking. I land with my feet in the sand, softly, with balance. Other nights I imagine watching television, usually a talk show, and I cannot understand why the guests on the show do not have Tourette. I think, How strange these people do not have the same movements and noises I do. I snapped out of my daydream as David said something quite incredible: "Do you ever think there is a little man in your brain, telling you when to Tourette and when not to?" Some of his comments were condescending, and he finally said the thing I hate most.

"I pity you."

"I don't need it," I responded quickly. Given David's attitude, I was curious to find out what he thought of my marital difficulties.

"In your country, women have too much freedom. They go from man to man. It should not be this way. Come to my country. I will introduce you to young women. They will go with you no matter where you travel. They will cling to you like a tick. An African woman will stay by the man's side. They know he is head of the household, whether he is a drunk or a ganja smoker, it does not matter."

I was somewhat surprised at this cultural difference and the manner in which women were viewed.

"In my country," David continued, "you can have two or three women in your bed. In the same bed to keep you warm at night. One on either side—fucking all night. They do not have desire to go from man to man, from this one to that one. They are cut at birth, this is the way it should be, like a dog is cut when it is young."

I was shocked at David's reference to female circumcision. Cutting a girl's clitoris sounded barbaric and I wasn't aware this was still a common practice in many African countries.

I tried to drift off to sleep that night next to Susanna, and I wondered if there was at least some aspect of truth in what David said. Of course not concerning female mutilation, but I did question our free-for-all society, our disposable, if-it-doesn't-work-throw-it-away attitude. Neither Susanna nor I seemed willing to sacrifice and compromise enough to make our marriage work. Would it be easier to separate and give up our union?

Susanna seemed so distant and I felt unable to focus, unable to be her partner in life. All we shared and worked for receded into a distant past with miscommunication or lack of communication increasing each day. Susanna hardly spoke, and I recited stoned nonsense, echoing her father's monologues. I felt as if my most important relationship was slipping away, and I didn't know what action to take. I stayed awake for a long time that night, trying to decide if I was really ready to give up with Susanna, or if she was willing to give up on me.

As a result of my behavior, Susanna built a wall around herself. It was a Catch-22. The more Susanna reacted to me in a closed-off fashion, the more I continued carrying on at friends' houses and smoking. The more I became reckless the more Susanna retreated from our partnership.

We bought a house in a wooded section of town within walking distance of the main street, and spent months fixing it up and making ourselves at home. The purchase of the house was exciting, and for a time distracted us from the widening rift in our marriage. I made a darkroom in the finished basement, and Susanna put together an office for herself. We were comfortable, but our relationship was on a downward spiral.

Susanna gardened and I got stoned. I worked in the darkroom stoned; talked on the phone stoned; and spent time at Terry's getting stoned. Susanna was working twelve-hour days at her job and came home exhausted. I usually made dinner, while smoking and listening to rock music. I became loud and boisterous. Susanna read and went to bed early. Two years after we were married, Susanna and I began to discuss seeing a psychiatrist for counseling. Susanna had applied, through her work, to attend a month-long workshop in Boston at the John F. Kennedy School of Government, a part of Harvard University. After being accepted, she made plans to spend June away, which I used to steep myself in a deep marijuana stupor.

One night I had a frightening dream that Susanna and I divorced and I became homeless in New York City. When I awoke I was alone and sweating profusely. Susanna had become in part my caretaker. I was not earning much money and worried about becoming immobile from a combination of severe Tourette and desperation. I washed my face, as if I could wash away my nightmare, dressed, and went out for a jog.

I felt the burden of what I dreamed the previous night, and the weight of my two-hundred-pound frame, as I jogged precariously on the dirt road that cut through a thickly wooded area. I wondered if separation would be a mistake. Should we stay together and try to work things out or was the marriage a mistake in the first place? The stark realization I came to was that there was no realization at all. I still did not know the answer to this question. Unable to reconcile with myself or Susanna, I felt lost.

# 9. Twitch and Shout

It was the morning of Inauguration Day 1989, and I was watching the proceedings on television when I received a phone call from Laurel Chiten, a documentary producer. She said she was in New York from Boston and asked if we could meet for lunch. That meeting was the beginning of a five-year odyssey for us both that resulted in the groundbreaking documentary about Tourette, *Twitch and Shout*.

"I really didn't know where I was going with this," Laurel recalled about that first encounter. "As we talked you were touching me, and I felt this immediate intimacy with you, like family. I don't know where it came from, but I remember turning to you and asking, 'Do you want to make this film with me?' There was just something about you that I thought would be a nice match."

Recently I asked Laurel, who has Tourette, to explain how she came to make a movie about it.

"I was plagued by these symptoms, such as neck twisting and jerking, which got progressively worse through my twenties," she explained, "but I was not diagnosed with Tourette until I was twenty-eight. I was annoyed that it took me so long to find out what was happening. I remember thinking, I'm working in television, I'm in a position to do something about this, so I knew I wanted to do something dramatic. I certainly didn't want to do a documentary, but I didn't think moviegoers were ready for a dramatic film about Tourette syndrome. The world needed to know what it was first. So I said okay, I'll make a documentary.

"I was sitting in my bathtub with a cordless phone, and my friend was telling me she was in the doctor's office and saw this *Life* magazine article called 'The Divine Curse,' written by Dr. Oliver Sacks. It talked about a community in northern Canada where they all have Tourette, and they were calling it Tourettesville. So I said, There's my story. I'm going to do a film on Tourettesville. I remember going to the library and reading it over and over again. There was this guy in the article named Lowell Handler who Dr.

Sacks traveled with, and it said he smashed his camera lens from Tourette. I thought this was the most bizarre thing I'd ever heard. You have to understand I didn't know that much about Tourette. I was afraid to meet you.

"I was supposed to be producing a big [television] show, and it was canceled. So I had some downtime. I took some of the channel's stationery and I typed Oliver Sacks a letter. I told him about the film I wanted to do, and also said I was a sign language interpreter, because I knew he was writing a book about the deaf. He wrote me back quickly. I don't know if there were misspellings, but there was certainly something wrong with his typewriter. He told me he also sent a copy of the letter he sent me to the Tourette Syndrome Association. Then Sue Levi from the Tourette Syndrome Association called me and said please come to New York to talk about it. I had a meeting with them and they said if you really want to do this you should meet Lowell Handler. Sue said, 'I'm warning you he has pretty severe Tourette.' "

From that beginning Laurel and I, with a small crew, traveled and videotaped *Twitch and Shout,* over a period of five years. Laurel was the director, producer, and writer of the film while I worked as the on-camera "Tourettic" host, narrator, and associate producer. In the film, which eventually was shown on public television, Laurel and I introduce the audience to the experience of Tourette through the lives of four main characters with extremely varied lifestyles: a Mennonite lumberjack from Alberta, Canada; an actress and singer from New York City; an artist, sculptor, and karate master from Toronto; and an NBA player for the Denver

*David Janzen and I became close friends during the time I spent visiting his large family of Mennonites, many of whom were affected by Tourette.*

Nuggets. We made a very personal film with humor and humanity, looking at Tourette from the inside.

David Janzen is a tall man with a weathered face and a deep, resonant voice, and the oldest of those we interviewed.

LaCrete, a Mennonite farming village in northern Canada, is David's home, where he and his family have lived for generations. Since David was the subject of the story Oliver Sacks and I did for *Life*, I had been to LaCrete a couple of times and was familiar with David and his family. In *Twitch and Shout*, David related an incident to which many Touretters could identify. His voice was shaky and as the camera zoomed in slowly for a close-up, tears began to well in David's eyes. He did not know he had Tourette during his teenage years when he was teased and tormented by classmates.

"I remember one time I was going to wrap a little present for someone. And it was quite fragile. And I broke the thing while I wrapped it. I was so upset, you know." Face-to-face with the camera, David was vulnerable and sincere. "In my kitchen, I have a set of knives on a shelf. I looked at those knives and thought, Which is the best one to get that devil out of me? But I couldn't. Instead I broke down and cried. Many, many times I've had those ideas."

David was on disability income for close to ten years because no one was willing to hire him. When we visited him, he had secured a full-time job in a lumber mill and machinery shop. David has managed to remain gainfully employed in the years since our film. I spoke with him last

Christmas and he told me all was well and that many of his relatives in the small village of LaCrete viewed our film on television.

The film also features Desiree Ledet, a very attractive actress, who is shown rehearsing and singing. She talks about Tourette from a different perspective. She has a facial tic, a shifting of her eyebrows, that is barely noticeable but is an uncontrollable impediment to her. Desiree grew up in the south and was teased in grade school. I thought it was interesting that Desiree chose a profession where she is literally and figuratively on stage, given the very observable movements of Tourette.

"When people can't see something visually it's hard for them to accept it. . . . When you're growing up and you have other children mimicking you, blinking literally in your face and calling you 'blinky' and 'winky' and names like that, it does affect you emotionally. It affects you throughout your life. When you have a parent, when you are sitting in church or at the dinner table and trying to concentrate so very much on not doing this, but you can't help it. And they slap you over and over and tell you to stop, and you know you can't stop. My mother didn't know what Tourette syndrome was at the time."

Desiree's beautiful voice and often touching stage performances are in stark contrast to her view of herself as imperfect. Her comments in our film are heartfelt and give insight into what it feels like to be outcast as a child.

Another subject, Shane Fistell, is an accomplished painter and sculptor

The artist Shane Fistell feels a strong connection to wild horses, which appear often in his work.

and works very diligently at his art. On camera we see Shane painting his signature images of wild horses, creating his works with broad, energetic strokes, and we watch as he molds a bust of a woman who sits patiently before us. Shane has severe Tourette, rarely resting for more than a moment in one place, and he sculpts the clay with frenetic movements. Occasionally pieces of clay fly onto the floor and Shane retrieves them, runs with lightning speed to touch a corner of the room off camera, and returns to finish smoothing the sculpture's surface in an oddly fluid motion.

Shane is a dashing and athletic young man, quite charismatic with his wild black hair and quick wit. He speaks poignantly about being stigmatized with Tourette:

"People, when they get drunk, go down the street hollering, screaming, fighting," he comments. "It may be frowned upon but it's not unacceptable. Drunken behavior is tolerated by society, whereas my tics are not. They are seen as something aberrant, something different, something strange." Shane tells a story about being asked to leave a movie theater because of Tourette, even after explaining his condition to the usher. "They can attack you physically, emotionally, try to humiliate you, and try to justify it. Always they are the victims of *my* Tourette."

Shane is irreverent and angry in the movie, often displaying his sharp wit. "Horses twitch too, you know," he says to me while painting the animal in vivid yellow and red colors. Shane resembles James Dean but with far more energy than the allegedly narcoleptic actor possessed. With his sardonic humor and energy-infused swagger, Shane brings Touretting to a high art.

At the time we interviewed him, Chris Jackson was a professional basketball player with the Denver Nuggets, though no bigger than five feet eleven inches tall. An African-American man who came from very modest beginnings and made a huge success as an athlete, Chris later converted to Islam and changed his name to Mahmoud Abdul-Rauf. He speaks about Tourette philosophically:

"There was an incident when I was in high school," he remembers. "I was in front of the mirror one day. I was doing it so bad, I was watching myself. I'm doing these movements. I had different motions at the time. I was there for such a long time, my whole body got sore. Please God, help me stop this. . . . I remember a line, I think from the Bible: 'For every infirmity God gives you a strength.' My weakness may be Tourette syndrome, but for my strength, He gives me basketball. That's how I'm able to cope with it."

Abdul-Rauf experiences many quick Tourettic sounds and movements that are often difficult to see on the basketball court because they are virtually indistinguishable from the game's heightened state of activity. This incredible athlete integrates Tourette into the sport's normal flow of action and noise in a way that is unnoticeable. And he may have even benefited from the symptoms of OCD, which accompany Tourette. In the film, Chris talks about staying an extra hour or two after practice until the ball "feels right" coming off his hands, endlessly repeating his shots. I'm sure that this perfectionism has helped him earn the title of NBA free-throw champion.

Mahmoud Abdul-Rauf (formerly Chris Jackson) has learned to integrate Tourettic rhythms, grunts, and movements into his game.

I could relate to the people we interviewed, particularly David Janzen, who didn't find out about Tourette until adulthood. Because I was in front of the camera presenting the interviews, those featured in the film felt comfortable revealing their lives. I obviously have Tourette and share many of the experiences that were discussed. The subjects in the film and I identified strongly with each other.

■ ■ ■

One of the highlights of the film was the Tourette Syndrome Association National Conference, which is held biannually, always in a different city. Hundreds of Touretters and their families converge from all over the world to talk, hold seminars on better serving the association's constituency, have scientific symposiums, and generally twitch out for a period of three glorious days.

Arrangements are made with the hotel of choice long in advance, and notices are sent to staff and guests so they are aware of the bizarre antics that will unfold during this weekend.

During the filming of *Twitch and Shout* the convention was held in the McLean, Virginia, Hilton, just minutes outside Washington, D.C. In the vast and lavish lobby I heard a woman say, "My son has full-blown Tourette, ADHD [attention deficit hyperactivity disorder, which is what used to be called ADD], OCD, and ODD [oppositional defiance disorder]." The last acronym, she explained, was doing the opposite of what the parent says and acting out, often in a sexual way. I thought, My God, this kid has alphabet soup. I was also amazed there was a category with which I was not familiar. At the opposite end of the room was a woman walking around yelling repeatedly, "I have AIDS I really do, gonorrhea, and syphilis too." Then she would switch to "Prozac's for prudes." Among this general mayhem, hoots, hollers, and birdcalls could be heard virtually any time of day or night.

Although hundreds were in attendance there were a few people in particular with whom I really wanted to speak. I found these individuals interesting because of decisions they had made in their lives that had been influenced by Tourette. Paige Vickery is a classical flutist and conductor in Denver; Jay Goodman, an inner-city firefighter in Pittsburgh; and Jeff Vitek and Cindy Bennett, a young couple from Tucson—both have Tourette and are engaged to be married.

Paige explained to me, "I was diagnosed at nineteen, my first year of college, and I am twenty-eight now. My sister called me about something she had seen on television. 'I think you might have something you can't control,' she said, which never occurred to me. I always thought it was something I was doing out of a lack of self-control. It's like your brain is involuntarily making you do things. I'm making myself do this so I must be able to stop it as well. I went to a neurologist and sure enough he said I have Tourette syndrome.

"I have head jerks and eye blinks all the time. And I have other different tics. I work freelance as a flutist and I conduct. I've guest-conducted in Europe and all over this country. If I thought about it I could always find something that [Tourette] irritates. Right now in my career I take on a lot of responsibility. I get up in front of an orchestra with eighty people waiting to get instruction and hundreds of people waiting to hear what they've paid for. When I concentrate Tourette goes away. I don't notice it goes away, it just does. If I put my baton down, there is silence, not a sound in the house.

"As we are growing up, we never analyze who we are as children, what we are doing, and what impact it's going to have, what lessons we are going to learn. Tourette must have taught me understanding, patience, and being open-minded. I practice more, I'm more organized because of the obsessive-compulsive thing. Perhaps these traits would have been there without Tourette, I don't know."

Before I ended our conversation, I asked Paige one more

thing. If there was a little pill that would take away Tourette forever, would she take it?

"I would rather not have Tourette, but I probably would refuse it, simply because you have to be careful of what you wish for. What will it undo? It could take away part of who you are."

Jay is a man I have seen at conferences for ten years, and yet we have never really spoken one-on-one for any length of time. "My life is very bizarre," he tells me. "I'm a risk-taker, an adrenaline junkie. I like to brag that I am a professional firefighter. I hang glide, skydive, white-water raft, and ride a Harley. If it has excitement I will do it. My belief is that Tourette has something to do with it, but I don't know what. We like to 'push the envelope.' Go as far as you can without breaking." Jay recounted his turbulent life. "I'm a recovered alcoholic and drug addict, and I've been clean for fifteen years. I did it to excess, nothing in moderation. I did everything short of sticking a needle in my arm. I believed that if you didn't stick a needle in your arm you could not become addicted. I went through Vietnam, I went to Turkey. I tried the hippie bit. I tried everything to fit in, not knowing what I had, just wanting to be accepted by people. I was about thirty-one or -two when I was diagnosed. I've accepted it, I'm doing OK, I'm very open about it. I keep a card with the saying 'To those who have experienced it, no explanation is necessary. To those who haven't, no explanation will do.' That's the truth. People can be sympathetic or identify with it a little bit, but they can't understand it."

Jeff and Cindy are the youngest people I interviewed at the conference. Both in their early twenties, they met at boarding school when they were teens. "We recognized that we both had Tourette and started talking about it," Jeff said. "I had been diagnosed when I was eighteen, she was about seven when she found out. I didn't know what it was growing up, she did."

"My mom always said, 'I understand, I understand,'" Cindy told me. "No, you don't, I thought. I can, he can. We're having children. If they have Tourette, who better to understand them growing up than us?"

"We'll know from the first sign," Jeff continued. "We'll be able to explain it to them. There is a certain amount of guilt to do it to someone else, but at the same time we're not passing on something that can't be overcome. It's not going to go away by us not having kids. It's not going to discontinue. It's like throwing all your trash in the garbage and expecting there to be no litter anymore. Having children is a big thing for us."

"If parents with Tourette have children," Cindy said, "we can teach them. They can learn from us and we can learn from our kids."

One of the highlights of the conference was a video-taped interview with Dr. Credo Mutwa of South Africa, who is a traditional Zulu healer. In full tribal garb, Mutwa spoke about his people's experience with Tourette: "There are seven diseases which our people regard as sacred diseases. We call them Isifo Samathongo—the diseases of the Gods. The disease that you described to me which you call Tourette syndrome is one of the two most sacred diseases in my people's culture. In olden days people who were victims of such diseases were either made into chiefs or kings or they were made into healers. . . . Another name for this disease is Indiki. The word Indiki means the pulse, the great pulse or jerk illness. The victims usually suffer from the jerking of the head, the strange and illogical sounds that this person makes, and sometimes . . . the person will let fly with the most horrendous swear words in Zulu."

I thought the words from the Zulu doctor were astonishing. How could a condition identical to one that people are ostracized for be exulted in another culture?

The videotape had quite an impact at the conference. We are accustomed to negative stigma, certainly not the religious reverence of Dr. Mutwa and his culture. Tourette may be viewed as a special power or a disability, but never anything in between. This disorder invokes strong feelings because it challenges that which is acceptable. In my experience, the Dutch have a great understanding and acceptance of "difference." This was demonstrated on my journey with Oliver Sacks, who attributed it to the philosopher Baruch Spinoza, with his emphasis on diversity and inclusion, and the Dutch history of tolerance and moral space. Conversely, the Japanese consider behavior such as touching or twitching an assault on decorum. In every language, Touretters tend to gravitate toward just those words and phrases that are most taboo, unable to suppress the very words that are forbidden in any particular culture.

It was a very enlightening weekend, and Laurel and I got a great deal of material for the film. But I came away with much more than just footage. I realized that this phenomenon has potential for an incredible bonding opportunity with other people, those with Tourette as well as those without. People who live with the condition of being different, whatever form that takes, have come to accept that which binds us in the human condition, rather than emphasize the difference.

Many people were eager to participate in the film, and

there are many with Tourette across the country and around the world who are eager to tell their stories of the misunderstanding and lack of compassion toward us. People everywhere have quirks and idiosyncrasies and often feel isolated because of these problems. The community that comes together every two years for the conference exists on a Tourettic continuum all the time, yet we live day to day with family, coworkers, and within a culture in which we stand out as "afflicted." Tourette may not be as rare or unique as previously thought, and I believe there is a large population who would want to understand us better once they see where we connect to them.

As *Twitch and Shout* ends, I share my thoughts. "I've learned a lot from these people. We are friends from the moment we meet because of a shared experience. It's an experience of constant being, a sense of excitement and stimulation. It's also an experience of being misunderstood constantly, sometimes of being stigmatized. At least now I know I'm not alone."

■  ■  ■

If the film was an adventure and somewhat therapeutic for me, it was difficult for Laurel. "It was an extremely hard film for me to make for a number of reasons," she recalls.

"I didn't have money, but the main problem was the subject matter. Tourette has been the hardest thing for me to deal with in my life. I can't say making a film about it was a catharsis. It was not. It got me closer to people's pain, where I saw my own pain mirrored."

Knowing that the film presented an opportunity to explain Tourette to many people who had never encountered twitchers before, Laurel felt the additional burden of representing an entire group of people. "I felt very responsible to [everyone] with Tourette," she continues, "and specifically to the people in my film, to present both a realistic and positive image of living with Tourette. I knew I was doing something that hadn't been done before. I wasn't just trying to construct an interesting film," she argues, "but one that showed a lot of care and love. I felt a lot of responsibility and fear—what if I did a bad job, or I hurt somebody, or misinterpreted something? I had a lot of pressure."

The five-year ordeal from our first meeting, through the conception of the film, the production, and editing, left us both tired and somewhat depressed. When *Twitch and Shout* was completed, we had no commitment from a television channel to air the program, nor did we have any idea where the hour-long documentary would be accepted for screening. Laurel was heavily in debt from production costs. In the beginning the travel and filmmaking process was exhilarating, but after a couple of years it became tedious and burdensome. Laurel often had to coerce me to tape segments in between other projects. I was confident we would have a compelling film in the end but was frustrated at how long the process was taking. I had faith in Laurel's fortitude and determination to see the project through but my patience wore thin. I kept trying to set my sights on the end result, the finish of this long journey.

■  ■  ■

Months later the film was complete and we had finally attained our goal. We had hoped to reach a national audience, but we were not prepared for the final outcome. *Twitch and Shout* was shown at the Museum of Modern Art and Lincoln Center in New York City, and won best documentary at the San Francisco International Film Festival. The film received the highest ratings of the season on public television's national prime-time *P.O.V.* series and in 1996 was nominated for an Emmy. Laurel and I attended the ceremony with pride and satisfaction.

# 10. A Second Chance at Life

**M**y work on *Twitch and Shout*, **and the re-action to the film, made it easier for me to ignore my personal problems and the continuing disintegration of my marriage.** I had done a great deal of traveling for the film, which had allowed me to put my own problems out of my mind, but at last Susanna and I had drifted too far apart, partly due to my escalated marijuana use, and in some part due to my wife's inability to connect to me emotionally. I continued to use pot as a crutch in dealing with everyday situations—before a train ride, the movies, or any social interaction I wanted to make easier. Marijuana greatly lessened my symptoms and self-medication was simple. I smoked pot numerous times a day and was stoned virtually all of the time. The days and nights at Terry's house or other neighbors' in Cold Spring were spent in adolescent activity, where we would carry on for days eating hashish brownies, drinking liquor, playing croquet, or having water-gun battles. Susanna was more and more disturbed by this behavior and the lack of communication between us. My life spun increasingly out of control. Susanna had taken the assignment at the John F. Kennedy School of Government, and I think she was glad to get out of town for a while, and away from me.

In spite of the problems between us there were intermittent good times as well, like a Jewish wedding we both enjoyed together. Two friends, Hannah and David, both of whom have Tourette, were married on a sunny spring day with a rabbi who was a friend of the two families presiding. The ceremony and reception were held in an elegant restaurant in Westchester, just north of New York City.

Hannah has a very mild case of Tourette while David's is more severe. He has what I call a "neurological stream of unconsciousness." David spoke Tourettic sentences, or entire monologues, in response to communication going on around him. This became exacerbated during formal, more tense situations such as his wedding day.

"We are filled with happiness today," the rabbi began, "as David and Hannah welcome us and the Tourette Syndrome Association, which has brought these two people together, and which this couple has given so much to—"

"Like money, money," David shouted. For each sentence the rabbi said, David had a comic response. After a while, the crowd came to expect a retort to follow the cleric's words.

"The things in life we all look forward to—" the rabbi continued.

"Grateful Dead tapes, Grateful Dead tapes," David added.

This Tourette "response" is not so unusual. I have known a number of people who manifest similar symptoms. Many of us in the room chuckled at David's outlandish comments, but as his friends and family we also understood.

As the band played, people danced and rejoiced. Susanna enjoyed the festivities, even if a little surprised at David's outbursts. My wife and I seemed happy during gatherings of large groups where we were not left to each other's company alone. One side of the building was glass and looked onto a beautiful lawn and garden. Over one hundred people attended, and everyone seemed to have a good time.

I dreaded the thought of staying in Cold Spring alone. While Susanna was away in Boston I became despondent at our distance from each other, physically as well as emotionally. I smoked from morning until night. One summer evening around five o'clock I was supposed to pick up Susanna's pet rabbits, which friends were caring for in her absence. It was rush hour, and I knew the roads were very busy. In spite of the fact that I was already stoned, I lit up another joint to calm myself just before heading out to the parkway. My car was in the shop so I used Susanna's Subaru.

My driving was tentative on this trip, because I was afraid to make any sudden moves. I managed to get to the parkway entrance without too much trouble, but at a stop sign with traffic fiercely whizzing by at sixty miles per hour, I didn't know how to find an opening to enter the flow of cars. I was confused and angry. Angry at Susanna for being away, and angry at myself for being so affected by it. I pumped the brakes, as if to test the machinery I was driving. I looked to my right and saw a flood of traffic headed north. I saw a large car traveling fast in the closest lane. At that moment, and with impaired judgment, I gunned the

accelerator and made a left-hand turn into oncoming traffic. As soon as I entered the roadway I felt a tremendous
impact. The car spun sideways. The crash and crunching
sound of breaking glass and torn metal were muffled, and I
imagined my death was imminent. With the crashing and
pileup as background noise I drifted out of consciousness,
thinking about the time, as a teenager, I fell off my new
ten-speed bicycle one night on Furnace Dock Road. As I
lay near my bike, a woman had said to me, "Are you all
right?" Her car stopped just inches from my body in the
middle of a thoroughfare. I was covered with dirt and grass
and could barely walk, but I mumbled something and
made my way to a friend's house.

These memories flowed through my mind as a man,
an emergency worker, shook me in the mangled seat of
Susanna's car. When I next woke up I was unable to move
my legs or arms as the paramedics rescued me from the car.
Voices everywhere were asking me my name and address
over and over again. I was put on a stretcher and then in an
ambulance. The only thing I could feel was tremendous
pain in my hands, which were stiff and frozen. I lay in a
hospital room and X rays were taken of my whole body.
Once the doctors found I had no broken bones, I was officially released, even though I couldn't walk. I called the

friends I was supposed to meet about the rabbits, and they picked me up at the hospital. My body was so contorted it was excruciating to get into their car and then home to bed. I was so frightened. I could barely believe what had just happened.

The next morning I was awakened by a phone call.

"Hello, Lowell, this is Joyce. We met on the parkway last night." It was the woman whose car collided with mine. Why was she calling me, I wondered, filled with new dread. But she had called only to tell me this: "I believe that God has given us both a second chance at life, and I think we should make the most of it."

■ ■ ■

The next day I called Susanna at Harvard and told her what had happened. Her car was totaled and she was not happy. The car accident was the third in a year. Was I a "risk-taker," as Jay at the conference had confessed he was? I was alone in the previous two car accidents and no one was hurt, but Susanna questioned my judgment. Although I was not stoned in the other accidents, they were also my fault. With the dope smoking, my careless attitude, and now this car accident, my marriage simply collapsed.

When Susanna returned home, we discussed separation in between appointments for MRIs and physical therapy. I had a spinal cord injury that required consultation with numerous neurosurgeons about the possibility of surgery. Susanna escorted me to all my doctors' appointments and helped me in the process of recovery, talking with me and the physicians at length. One of the neurosurgeons, at New York University Medical Center, advised us that with time I would recover, and that complex, risky, and expensive surgery was not the way to go. We decided to take his advice, the most conservative action, which was no action at all.

During the following winter I slowly recovered, even if my marriage did not. We cried in each other's arms often, but Susanna held the accident against me. I did not blame her. When, late one night, Susanna said, "I cannot do this anymore," I knew what she meant. We decided that when my brother, Evan, moved into his new uptown apartment, I would move to his old place in lower Manhattan, the same apartment where I had lived more than a dozen years earlier as a college student just diagnosed with Tourette.

I felt as if the only real union and love I had with a woman was falling out from under me. I didn't know if I would ever be able to walk properly or run again. I was scared and hurt. My whole life was collapsing.

Susanna and I were resigned to the idea of divorce and I

slowly packed boxes full of my belongings, separating my things from hers and sorting out the rest we had accumulated during three years of marriage. I felt I was leaving a safe haven, the stable comfort of my home and my wife. I moved out on April Fool's Day, the same day I had left my parents' house sixteen years earlier to travel and learn to better understand myself. Once again, I found myself facing an uncertain future.

■  ■  ■

Moving to New York's East Village on an early spring day, I was surprisingly exhilarated to see the old neighborhood once again. With the quick pace of people—motion everywhere—I realized I was back in my element. Punks with spiked orange hair mixed with drug-buying yuppies. Elderly Polish and Ukrainian women wearing babushkas and gingerly pushing shopping carts walked along the sidewalk with homeless people putting out their hands for money. Men in Armani suits with cell phones briskly turned the corner while revelers would be just returning home from a night's drinking. For a short time I was so entranced with the strong life force of the neighborhood that I didn't think that much about my separation from Susanna. I spent the next few days settling into my apartment and frequenting a coffee shop on lower Second Avenue.

At the Mission Cafe, a tiny, upbeat, brightly painted eatery and coffeehouse, I noticed an attractive young woman who was ticcing. I was reticent to approach her, but as we became aware of each other, I went to her table and introduced myself.

"I'm Jenny, sit down," she said. I asked Jenny if she had Tourette, and she explained that she had just been diagnosed a few months ago. She was a senior at a prominent New York art college, a painter who grew up in the suburbs. I was curious about her growing up, as I did, without knowledge of Tourette. I identified strongly with Jenny from this first meeting. Since both of us were diagnosed at the same time in our lives, we shared the mystery of Tourette. Jenny was pretty, and was honest in her account of her family's reaction to her disorder.

"For such a long time I've been dealing with these twitches and not knowing what they were," she explained. "My mom would think they were allergies, but why would that be an allergy? I tried to find a reason.

"When I was in first grade, my teacher would hassle me about my nose-wrinkling, sniffing twitch, and ask, 'What are you doing that for?' My teachers were a major influence on me, and I was the outcast," she recalls. "I didn't have any friends, but I once was invited to this party. It was for

Allison, it was her party, and they put me under the pool table and poked me with pool cues without letting me out. It seems like such a far-out torture, I'm horrified when I look back at it.

"When I moved from private Catholic school to public school I was ten, and I had a lot of different tics," she continued. "Huffing and puffing, twitching my head, and worst of all my neck. Every single boy made fun of me, except one who liked me. He made fun of me one day, and he apologized. He saw my face. It made me feel like a romance, even though I was ten years old. It's like I had seen it in one of those ABC afterschool specials.

"I had the lowest self-esteem, but I'm very confident now. If someone makes fun of me I just tell them it's just something I do. Don't make fun of something I can't control; that's not fair. It's like making fun of me for having brown eyes.

"I'm also hyperactive, so I jump around. They took me to the school psychologist in fifth grade. He just thought I was a nervous kid. He recorded these really monotone, irritating, relaxation sessions.

"When I was in my second year of college, I was raped by a friend of mine. When I went to the district attorney, I couldn't finish my sentences because I was too busy huffing and twitching. My father yelled at me, and I said, 'If you ever paid attention you would know I've had this for years. I can't control it.' He does understand, he was just frustrated. I have such a short fuse, I don't like to take any shit."

Like many other Touretters, Jenny was faced with health professionals who sought to blame her condition on psychological causes. "I have gone through two therapists," she explained. "One telling me I was mentally and physically abused. I said no, I wasn't. I dumped her. I just wanted to talk about the twitches because I wanted to finally find out what they were. I was searching because they were beginning to overwhelm me. Then I saw a neurologist and found out what it was."

As Jenny talked, she became less inhibited: "I have a third nipple," she blurted out, "and I got it pierced, wanna see?" She lifted up her shirt. "My mother always said, 'If you want to wear a bikini we can get that removed.' I'm proud of it, this is my little baby. It's such a part of me.

"One thing Tourette has taught me is a lot of humility. I'm an honest, affectionate, and loving person. I've always been very social, I have too much energy not to be. Most people think it's cute. They think the huffing and puffing is cute. You feel like you don't have any secrets. These uncommon little deformities teach you so much. Like one of the things that help me accept my third nipple. It's nothing I should be embarrassed about.

"Another thing that I've found about people with Tourette, they are very affectionate, fun, easygoing. We've all been taught humility."

Jenny was more mature than I was and was handling her situation better. She seemed more at ease with herself and the new set of identity problems the permanence of Tourette brought with it. Although we were both seniors in art school when we were diagnosed, Jenny was now very self-assured and comfortable with herself as a Touretter and a woman. This self-confidence helped others to respond warmly to her. I also believe I was more depressed than she, which might be due to differences in our medication.

I realized that Jenny was the first woman I had met socially with Tourette out in public rather than through a support group or organization. I was reassured by our casual meeting and by her self-confidence. Though we had had a Tourette moment, we had also simply encountered each other as any two strangers would. I felt as if Jenny represented the pathway to my experiences with Touretters in the world at large.

Over the weekend I wandered around in order to reacquaint myself with the neighborhood. Vibrant young couples on respite from the week's work sat outside at cafés. Tall, leather-clad men with metal studs around their wrists and necks hung out on stoops around St. Mark's Place. Sexy women dressed in short skirts and high-heeled shoes walked dogs up and down tree-lined streets. Others, wearing all black clothing and heavy layers of makeup, resembled concentration camp victims in a modern-day setting.

Second Avenue just off St. Mark's Place looked like a Persian marketplace, with people selling every imaginable good—used clothing, telephones, kitchen utensils, and pornography—set out on blankets by street people trying to make ends meet. I imagined if one of the blankets could fly, its owner, a magic genie, and all of his belongings would be transported to another land. As I walked, the sky grew dark and a torrential rain began. Suddenly people were running for cover under awnings and against buildings. I found myself in a narrow doorway shoulder to shoulder with a young salesman. The man was holding an ordinary white business-size envelope, which was marked 50 cents.

"I'll let you have it for a quarter," he said, and I bought it. I ran home through the rain and as I sat at my kitchen table I opened the envelope. It contained a folded piece of paper, hand-lettered, that read:

> *Develop or create a chemical imbalance in your body.*
> *Find God.*
> *Recruit followers.*
> *Retire.*

At that moment I knew the East Village, with all its madness, was my home. I became one of the characters who inhabit these streets, these buildings. I was here to stay.

# 11. Tourette Culture

**F**or many years now, I had been preoccupied by the world of Tourette. Through my early work with the Orphan Drug Act and my collaboration with Oliver Sacks to my activities in the Tourette Syndrome Association and the shooting of the film *Twitch and Shout*, I had been thinking about how we view the world differently due to our Tourette. I had spent much time pursuing my own inner journey, and now I wondered what we as Touretters have in common with each other, and what is different about each of us. Could it be said that there was a distinctly unique "Tourette culture"?

Soon after I had settled into the East Village, I was presenting *Twitch and Shout* at a public screening in Manhat-

176

tan. After the program a strikingly beautiful young woman with long hair and piercing eyes approached me. She said her name was Ellen and extended her hand, twitching slightly. As we began talking she seemed shy but self-confident. We talked until most of the audience had gone, and before she left I said I would like to get together with her sometime. She handed me a slip of paper with her phone number written in tentative penmanship.

Over the next week we spoke on the telephone a couple of times, but one night Ellen called from a subway station near my apartment and I suggested she visit. It was late, but I wanted to see her. "You're sure it's OK?" Ellen asked. I had been thinking about her since we met a week earlier. Ellen seemed intelligent and particularly well read, but she had not been working for years, due to a disabling and extreme case of OCD. Her Tourette seemed minor compared to how she described her obsessive-compulsive disorder. Ellen received government assistance for living expenses because of this condition but was embarrassed and angry that she had to do so.

We talked that first night about our lives and books we had both read. It was not long, however, before we acknowledged we were very obviously attracted to each other. From the first, almost frantic embrace our months spent together were a Tourettically charged, intensely erotic affair.

It was a rare thing for me to meet someone with whom I formed an almost instant familiarity, a closeness and intimacy that contradicts good sense. This was the case with Ellen despite a bizarre set of difficulties. We were never able to meet at a specific time because it took Ellen hours to leave her apartment. These hours were theoretically composed of all kinds of rituals that she never really explained to me. One of the things Ellen did mention was that she had trichotillomania, which means she compulsively and uncontrollably pulled out her eyebrow hair. This was disturbing to her because she hated how it affected her appearance. I never witnessed Ellen's hair pulling and other, more "invisible" aspects of OCD were difficult to pinpoint. I never knew the specifics of her compulsions because she wouldn't discuss them with me. I suspect there were many of them, however, as this prevented us from leading a "normal" dating life.

Visits to my apartment continued. Ellen would not tell me where she lived, nor would she allow me to visit her apartment, which she told me was one room filled with leftover food, and a general mess. She told me she had a fear of touching food, a fear that caused her to deprive herself of eating for twelve to twenty-four hours at a time. Mornings at my apartment often included Ellen locking herself in the bathroom for two hours. In many respects, Ellen was an urban hermit, venturing outside only to shop or sleep with me. Much of our relationship existed over the telephone. Ellen always had her answering machine on to screen calls, but she would pick up the receiver once she heard my voice. Ellen also developed telephone code names for us. I'd hear on my machine, "Ben Yahoota, this is Maximum Bob calling. Tourette Boy, this is Tourette Girl on the line."

Our evenings together were forays into intense sexual exploration. Ellen would arrive looking pretty and in a good mood. "Hi, how ya doing," she'd greet me. We would be entwined and undressing before she came through the doorway. Our sexual improvisations were frank and torrid, no holding back. We would collapse after hours of some passionate game-playing and sleep soundly. But alone in my apartment I wondered if our shared Tourettized language and its erotic expression were enough to sustain the relationship. Ellen never wanted to go out anywhere and it seemed as though all our communication, sexual or otherwise, was characterized by our Tourettisms.

Despite my attraction to Ellen, I found I didn't want a

relationship with someone who was not really capable of functioning in mainstream society. It worried me I might be guilty of the same bias other women might direct toward me. Perhaps I was thinking less of Ellen in the same manner other girlfriends had thought less of me because of my "differences." I found it naturally difficult to partner with a "disabled person," someone victimized by Tourette, and recalled my fright at spending time with other Touretters whose symptoms were more seriously debilitating than mine. Ellen had become increasingly resentful of my involvement with publicizing the disorder, dubbing me the "King of Tourette." When I discussed how I hoped the book I was writing would be informative but also entertaining, she became angry. "Entertainment, huh? Go to the hospital and look at people who are chronically sick, see if you can laugh at that.

"You're a Tourette pimp," she accused, "and I'm sick of it. Put that in your book."

■ ■ ■

As I pursued my professional career, I was quite aware that my disorder separated me from other photographers and editors, but I refused to allow this difference to become a quarantine. I wanted to prove to myself, and others in my field, that I could function as well as anyone else. I was to make one of my most interesting professional connections several years ago at a prestigious conference at the Maine Photographic Workshop in a small town on the Maine coast.

This was an opportunity to meet photography editors from major magazines and have work critiqued by them. During the three weeks I spent in Rockport, Maine, I met Don McCullin, a famous British war photographer. Don had published *Is Anyone Taking Notice*, a landmark book that brought public awareness to war-torn situations and suffering around the world. McCullin told me that he knew another photojournalist who had Tourette. "He's in Paris and has done some work for *Newsweek*. You should speak to Robert Pledge. He knows how to get in touch with this man."

I found Robert Pledge at the workshop getting ready for a wine reception and introduced myself. Robert is the owner of Contact Press Images, a New York- and Paris-based photography agency that covers news events for publication. Robert did indeed know Jean-Claude Labbé, a fellow Frenchman and photojournalist with Tourette syndrome. "He spends a lot of time in Vietnam," Robert said. "I'll tell you how to reach him when we get back to New York."

Upon returning to New York I followed up with Robert who told me Jean-Claude often came to New York and offered to help us meet. When I spoke to Labbé over the phone, it turned out he was fluent and Tourettically cursed in three languages: French, Vietnamese, and English. He had a fascination with Asian culture and had been photographing in Vietnam since the early seventies when he published a breakthrough piece in *Newsweek*, which he authored and photographed.

The following autumn Jean-Claude was to make a trip to New York. Coincidentally, the Maine Photographic Workshop was having an awards ceremony at Nikon House, located in Rockefeller Center. I had submitted and received an honorable mention for my piece on Orrin Palmer, the doctor with Tourette syndrome. When I got to Nikon House, I asked Robert if Jean-Claude was there yet. "You'll know when he's here," Robert said. At that moment I heard a loud mouth-popping noise, followed by what sounded like someone yelling. Jean-Claude had arrived.

He was a short man who flailed his arms and legs, outstretched and jerking, as he walked. Jean-Claude came equipped with cameras dangling from his neck, constantly clicking his loud Nikon, which added to the symphony of his noises. It seemed as though Jean-Claude integrated gesticulation, as if it were punctuation, into his repertoire of speech and motion.

We met and introduced ourselves, and with a distinct French accent he said, "I am the French version of you American twitchers." We had a good laugh, but had to settle down as it was time for the awards ceremony. My friend and agent, Howard Chapnick, was presenting, and the crowd was gathering around to listen. As the room became quiet and Howard began to speak, the loud noises Jean-Claude and I made became increasingly noticeable. What was worse was that the more Jean-Claude was Touretting, the more I made noises and twitched. This "copy-cat" Touretting is typical when groups of people with Tourette get together. We tend to set each other off on a relay of symptoms.

The public relations man from Nikon said to Robert, "Your friends are making too much noise. They must be drunk or something. If they do not stop, we are going to have them removed."

"Oh no, you don't understand," Robert said. "This is a disease, they can't help it."

"Both of them have it?" the man from Nikon asked incredulously.

After the formality of the ceremonies Jean-Claude and I

decided to hail a cab for Chinatown, Jean-Claude's favorite part of New York City. People in this cramped, small-scale neighborhood were perplexed by our symptoms. Some seemed angry and outraged by our behavior, others simply at a loss for an explanation. We walked around Touretting and smelling the great Chinese delicacies for what seemed like hours, until we found a place Jean-Claude knew. When we entered the restaurant, we were seated by a friendly waiter who could not help noticing our "strangeness." The two of us ordered a wonderful feast and as we ate, the waiter asked, "Were you guys in the war?"

Jean-Claude had a different attitude about public reaction to Tourette than me. Whereas I explained it to anyone who inquired, he refused to offer an explanation.

The next day I dropped Jean-Claude off at Kennedy Airport for his return flight. We had lunch at a café while waiting for him to board the plane. Amid kicking and barking, the waitress said, "Are you two all right?"

"We are high on crack!" Jean-Claude quickly responded.

"No," I said. "We both have a neurological disorder."

"I believe him," the waitress said, pointing to me.

■　■　■

Since medieval times, people with deformities and "differences" overcompensated for their oddities with an acute sense of humor and play. This self-deprecation could result in a job as court jester or circus performer, but the roles of wise man and fool have frequently been interchangeable. Starting in childhood a highly developed sense of humor often accompanies Tourette, ADD, and learning disabilities. Early displays of antic behavior are the beginning of a life spent trying to "fit in" to a society where there is little acceptance for nonconformity.

Recently I found an essay on the Internet by George Lynn, a mental health counselor who works with children. He calls these kids "Attention Different," and writes: "Living open to experience, they inhabit the Fool or Shaman archetype. In times of crisis those who have weird qualities will emerge to help people through change. At this time in our evolution, when all the conventional answers seem to be failing, we see the emergence of our 'weird' in these strange kids with their strange abilities and excesses of character. Because just as Attention Different kids have 'crazy artistic' or 'little anarchist' temperament challenges, they also possess rare gifts in their weirdness. We need [these gifts] to survive, as people, as we go into the twenty-first century."

To what extent this "otherness" exhibited by people with ADD (ADHD), Tourette, or OCD is caused by external, environmental factors is also addressed. George Lynn goes on to say, "My own son, a bright ten-and-a-half-year old, has Tourette syndrome. His condition came about partly as a result of my exposure to Agent Orange in Vietnam twenty-four years ago. Some good research out of Stanford is suggesting that environmental insult can potentiate emergence of abnormal neurological conditions." I have met several people with Tourette who first experienced symptoms after a life-threatening or emotionally traumatic event in their life. My friend Rose Rogers had a terrible fall from a galloping horse when she was fifteen years old. She was unconscious for several days, and later awoke in the hospital and began to experience the symptoms of Tourette. Whether Tourette can be caused by environmental factors is unclear; however, there is strong evidence in this overpopulated, overpolluted world that we are all susceptible.

When I shared this essay with my father, he reminded me of the talks we had when I was young and had no idea why I acted so differently from others.

"I used to say to you, 'Don't feel strange, this is the future.' People like you are vehicles to get us across into the next stage. And this changeover will result in people with large heads, bulging eyes, and no hair. They will have jet propulsion strapped on their backs, like Buck Rogers. And their bodies will be very small because of what the atmosphere has done to us, what we have done to our planet. You are taking it on the chin for what we as a people have done for money and 'progress.' "

Maybe, though my father's theory isn't widely acknowledged. I do not know if there is a connection either between "Attention Difference" and genius or creativity. Van Gogh may well have had epilepsy. Oliver Sacks has written a piece in the *British Medical Journal* exploring the possibility that Mozart may have had Tourette. I think it is simply that my population exists in greater numbers than was previously thought. I am convinced that among all the Earth's cultures, parallel, above, or beneath, there exists a distinct Tourette culture.

# 12. Crazy and Proud

**I**n thinking about human "difference," I realize that I am not unique. Many people experience far more extreme departures from normality than those of Tourette syndrome. Mental illness can cause people to hallucinate—hear things and see things that are not actually there. Whose reality is genuine? In addition to the way Tourette changes my perception of reality, it also changes that reality itself: other people's reactions to me, and my reactions to their reactions. Why is one person called "crazy" and another "neurologically impaired"? Perhaps I too was one of the crazy people. I would find out by immersing myself in their world.

■ ■ ■

Cobblestone Road is a building on New York's Lower East Side, in a section of the city set apart from the fast-paced financial district it borders. In the early 1900s, Cobblestone Road was a hospital. Tuberculosis was rampant and thought to "live" in the corners of buildings, so this hospital was built with bay-sided semicircles forming the two halves of the structure, giving the virus no purchase. Superstition and misinformation about the disease were abundant, as they would later be about Tourette syndrome and many other medical conditions. I came to this historic building made of brick and stone to work with the homeless mentally ill.

Community Access, the nonprofit organization that operates Cobblestone Road, provides housing, food, job training, and social work services to low-income, homeless women and men with psychiatric histories. Even though the agency has numerous buildings with supervised housing, Cobblestone is unique—a self-contained community where tenants have a permanent home. This arrangement includes a lease with all legal privileges and responsibilities due any tenant in the city of New York. Within Cobblestone's walls is a complete kitchen, dining area, office, recreation center, and over one hundred studio apartments. Cobblestone remains representative of an ideal, where people recovering from all kinds of difficulties can live without fear of losing housing, or any infringement on their lifestyle, provided they do not break the law.

In 1994, after separating from Susanna, I was broke and desperately needed a job, not to mention some positive work experience. I was also ready to give up pot. A family friend who worked at Community Access mentioned that a new facility was opening after undergoing a two-year renovation. I mailed a résumé then called, hoping for an interview. Within a number of weeks I had three interviews, the final one to meet the other members of this new staff. I was to become well acquainted with this social work "dream team."

The job I was offered was as a recreation therapist. I was thrilled to be employed but more than a little worried about working with this difficult population. I had experience working with mentally retarded people, as well as troubled children in rural residential settings. Cobblestone is an urban, inner-city setting acquainted with problems such as AIDS, prostitution, theft, drug addiction, and violence. During one of my interviews I was asked to speak with residents of other Community Access housing in addition to various staff. At one point, I asked a group of staff members if there was ever the threat of violence.

"It's very rare," a young female staffer told me, "most people usually—" At that moment a large woman smashed through the closed door screaming, "I'm gonna kill you, I'm gonna get you," and wrenched her hands around the neck of the woman who had answered my question. After the situation was defused we broke the tension by laughing at the ironic timing of this incident.

In spite of any misgivings I was intrigued. The management and staff looked to be sincere and experienced professionals. Gordon Hough, the director of the new program at Cobblestone, is a man in his fifties with white and gray hair pulled back in a ponytail and an extremely deep, gravelly voice. He has a Ph.D. in English literature, but had given up an academic, theoretical lifestyle for the practical world of social service and making a tangible difference in people's lives. Gordon managed every aspect of Cobblestone, both from his home computer via E-mail, and in weekly "team" meetings among staff. They were friendly and seemed truly interested in supporting each other, as well as the residents. I decided to take the job based on my favorable impressions of the people already working there.

My duties were to coordinate many activities on an optional basis, including theater, sports, board games, cards, community dinners, art, opera, and a weekly Friday-night party I dubbed the "soiree." I began work at Cobblestone before most tenants arrived. Many of the people served by Community Access were substance abusers, like me, and I concluded it would be inappropriate for me to continue smoking given this circumstance. I gave up weed "cold turkey," and immersed myself in Cobblestone Road for two and a half years.

One of the first people I met was a case manager named Angel. Case managers help tenants handle various aspects of their lives, whether it's paying a utility bill or personal problems that need counseling. This service, available to all, was offered only if desired by the tenant. As Angel extended his hand to meet me, I touched him Tourettically, followed by a loud grunt.

"I'm Lowell," I said. "I'm going to do activities here." Angel seemed curious about my Tourette, which I tried to explain.

"What did you say?" he asked. "You have 'jerk' syndrome?" I said no, I have Tourette syndrome, which he informed me was not familiar to him. We both laughed, and I was reminded of the expression "jerk illness," used by the Zulu healer I had seen at the Tourette Syndrome Association conference.

Angel is a robust man with a round, friendly face. His

family had come to New York from Puerto Rico and remained on the Lower East Side, not far from my apartment. Angel's jovial manner was not lost on even the most downtrodden resident who came downstairs to the office area looking for camaraderie. One such tenant was Lou, who was around thirty years old with a large frame. He wore baggy clothes and T-shirts with funny expressions imprinted across the back. Lou had a number of problems, including OCD. He often approached the staff joking about feeling dejected.

"I'm the opposite of gay, I'm depressed," Lou would say. "I'm depressed about some personal shit."

"They have something to enlarge it now," Angel would quip. This banter was especially common at the weekly Friday-night soiree, which Angel and I held together. After a long workweek, as most of the staff were preparing to go home, Angel and I would gather chips, dip, soda, and hors d'oeuvres for a rambunctious night of frivolity.

Lou had become increasingly obsessed with former Chief of Staff Alexander Haig, the CIA, and Israeli intelligence.

"Alexander," Lou would say as he saluted, Nazi style, and clicked his heals together, "the Great."

"Do you think Alexander Haig is a fascist, or maybe just conservative? You never know, you never know. Do you think he likes women or men? You never can tell with people like that—you know what I'm saying? He might have been a little funny. Do you think he takes drugs? I've done hard drugs: marijuana, heroin, cocaine, LSD, NutraSweet."

Two of the tenants who rarely missed a soiree were Barbara and Erwin, a couple who had been living at Cobblestone for three years. Barbara had OCD and schizophrenia and would discuss these painful afflictions in a chatty, self-deprecating way.

"I will mop the floor while Erwin is sitting at the table drinking a cup of coffee," she'd tell me. "I'm looking at the floor and ask, 'Should I mop it again? It looks dirty on that side of the room.' And I'll wait for Erwin to leave, and then sneak the mop out again. I can't stand for anything to be at the edge of the table. Even when I go to bed, I've got to check the door, lie back down, and then check the lock again. It's a pain. I have to do these things, my mind will not give me any peace until I do. Without the Prozac it was driving me up the wall. The Prozac has helped.

"I also have a psychiatric history," she explained. "I've been diagnosed as paranoid schizophrenic. But I also have skills. I am a word processor. I type—medical typing, shorthand. I've got to practice here in the computer room. I love computers and typing." As Erwin sat next to her, Barbara told me how she came to Cobblestone.

"I was homeless in a shelter for two years, getting robbed. I contracted HIV from a man, a creep I was involved with. I asked him to wear a condom. I used to beg the man to wear a condom. And he would say, 'What do you have?' And I'd tell him 'nothing.' After two months of having sex with this man, we brought up the subject of where the relationship was going, and he told me flat out that he was HIV positive. He knew it the whole time. I could have had him locked up, because today you can go to jail for that. I wasn't thinking along those lines. I was so hurt. I wanted to run out into traffic. I was told people are living ten or fifteen years with this HIV status. There are new drugs. My T cells are pretty high. It's scary. Very scary for me."

Erwin had met Barbara when he arrived at Cobblestone and said, "When she told me about the encounter with that man, it made me sick to my stomach. I couldn't handle it emotionally, him saying 'I got it, you got it now, babe.' That doesn't go with me. I raised two daughters.

"Prior to the time I came out of the shelter, I was working. Until I had an accident—a minor stroke. I lost my speech—everyone was happy. I had been married to a woman with a problem; she had Parkinson's. My young child had anorexia nervosa and OCD, and maybe even an episodic mood disorder. On top of that they diagnosed her with schizophrenia—it can't be. She heard a voice saying 'don't eat, don't eat.' All anorexics hear that voice. Schizophrenia is a mysterious disorder that hinges on chromosome number two, and dopamine. I did a lot of reading on the Internet about it. Also about your disease, Tourette.

"So I had the minor stroke, and I had to stop work. I finally ended up in a shelter."

"Being in a shelter, you don't have privacy," Barbara said. "Nothing like the freedom and privacy I get here at Cobblestone. When I first got here all I did was cry. It was like my own little dollhouse. It's mine. I wasn't ever going to be homeless again."

One day I was working in the office when Lou phoned from the psychiatric unit at Bellevue. He had admitted himself a few days earlier because of persistent, uneasy, and troubling thoughts.

"How are you, Lou?" I asked tentatively.

"Alexander!" Lou responded, and I could see, in my mind, old Lou's salute. "Not so great," he finished sadly.

■ ■ ■

My supervisor at Cobblestone was Teresa, a young woman with a serious attitude toward people and her work, but also with a good sense of humor. Teresa supervised a number of case managers at the building and often acted as a buffer between staff and residents. She had a great ability to ease potentially confrontational situations. Once, a six-foot-seven-inch-tall man who had been a former gang member became angered and was ready to attack when Teresa was able to apply her training in counseling. She had helped a terminally ill client gain a sense of acceptance and closure about his life. She had also ridden with paramedics in an ambulance to be close to a tenant needing hospitalization. Teresa had worked at numerous sites in New York with social service agencies that assisted homeless men and women. Both of her parents had come to this country from Puerto Rico and had to struggle with a new language and poverty in Spanish Harlem, where Teresa was raised. She worked hard, for many years, and overcame great obstacles as a member of a minority in this country. Recently Teresa completed a master's degree in social work. I asked her about how the tenants responded to my condition.

"Working with you was very interesting," she began. "I knew of your diagnosis, but when you start working with someone, you really see. I thought, Here I am complaining about this and that in my life, and you told me something about your daily life experiences with Tourette. The residents said, 'That's just Lowell.' At first they thought you were rather strange. What helped in terms of relating to the residents is that you were comfortable in explaining what this is all about. It was as if you said, 'This is what Tourette is like.' Your humor helped a lot. I can't totally put myself in your position, but I can understand to some extent."

At Cobblestone I learned that people can come from very diverse backgrounds with all sorts of problems and still live and work together. At times there was tension, however, and we all tried to accommodate each other in the best way we could. I also learned from Teresa the meaning of social work and empowerment. A social worker is not a curse word thrown around by Republican politicians. It is an honorable profession practiced with great patience and skill by overworked, highly undercompensated people possessing knowledge and compassion. Social work is about showing the people you encounter how they can use their skills to empower themselves in this world. Our job as social workers is to bring about change. And we've got to be realistic about what we can change.

Another tenant I talked to often was Ralph, who grew up on the Lower East Side and had been at Community Access for many years. A bearded man in his late thirties who usually carries a cup of coffee, Ralph is slow and serious. His studied speech rolls off his tongue gently but with conviction. Ralph had been fighting a battle with substance abuse—cocaine and alcohol—and was losing.

He was living on a bench during the Tompkins Square Park riot of 1988. Anarchists and skinheads were using the homeless as target practice for their anger and Ralph became caught in the crossfire.

There was no privacy in the park. Once in a while he'd go to a friend's house and take a shower. A woman on the steps of a clinic on Second Avenue gave him a card for Community Access. Ralph went to the address and found a man there who let him sleep in the classroom for a couple of hours. Afterward he received information about intake to the agency. After some time in a shelter, four months in a psychiatric hospital, and the Salvation Army, Ralph found himself at Community Access's first residence, called Libby House. At Libby he learned how to live again, how to take a shower, take medication. Ralph went on to get his high school equivalency diploma and scored high on the math. He took the peer-specialist program for training in entry-level work and got an internship through them.

Ralph took advantage of a Community Access recovery program called Double Trouble for MICA people (mentally ill chemically addicted), people who are dually diagnosed.

Ralph still attends Double Trouble today, but told me he's been clean for five years and three months. "I know where I am going," he now says, "I know where I came from, and I know what helped. It saved my life."

I asked Ralph how he felt about working with me and what he made of my Tourettic behavior. "You came here, you worked, you came to help people," he says simply. "At first I didn't understand the way you would just touch people, but it didn't look like you were hurting anyone. It didn't bother me that much. I'm a person who doesn't like to be touched, but with therapy and medication I can deal with that today. I enjoyed working with you here."

Angel and I held our Friday-night soirees for almost three years, a tradition that Barbara renamed "the sorry-ass soiree." Angel never stopped his good-natured teasing about my condition. "Let me get you an invention, Lowell, elastic bands tied from your wrists to your waist, so it will snap your hand back when you reach out to touch people. Or, you can attach business cards to your hand, so you can promote yourself while you're touching people." Angel also delighted in telling tenants about his misadventures with me.

"We jumped into a cab one time and the driver screamed, 'Don't touch me,' as if he was going to beat the living shit out of us. Sometimes people on the street will jump twenty feet in the air from the loud noises Lowell makes. They are petrified. Once on the subway, I thought Lowell was reaching for someone's nuts. I figured he would know how to handle it if something broke out. I know he handles it every day of his life." Angel would continue to tell people I had "jerk" syndrome, and I would tell people how he was my favorite minority.

Angel began telling me his family's story: "The Lower East Side is the only neighborhood I know. I don't even travel to the other boroughs. This guy approached my mom with a bat in one hand, and his house in the other [meaning he was homeless and moving with belongings from place to place]. My mom wiped his face with a towel, and she cleaned him up. He walked away sad. This guy returned a week later after going to the Salvation Army. He was through detox. He cleaned himself up and dressed just to thank my mom. She didn't even recognize him. It had been nine years since he had spoken to another human being. Robert was his name. He was the first manic depressive person I knew. He had been living underneath the FDR Drive in a pup tent. I brought him steak, beans, and rice during a hurricane. He called me 'Big Boss Man,' and he said, 'How do you know I'm not a killer? I've got more fleas than a pigeon. How do I know you are not a killer?' He never had anybody do this for him. From then on he was at every family occasion, even after my mother passed away.

"My mother's brother was diagnosed with schizophrenia at the age of seventeen. He had electric shock treatment. He died at fifty-four years old with the mind of a nine year old. We thought of people being off the wall or weird when I was a kid. We didn't really know it was called mental illness. My uncle hallucinated. There were street gangs then [in the seventies], and he hallucinated about a man with a bandanna and a machete going wild.

"Both my parents passed away. I had to wean my older brother off a respirator because he was a long-term survivor of AIDS. Some people say, 'I'm sorry for your loss,' but I look at them as my gains. A sense of humor allows you to laugh. Since life is rough it's better to laugh at some things. I feel it's made me stronger in a lot of ways because in spite of the tragedy, you have to move on with your life. A smart man learns from his mistakes, but a wise man learns from others' mistakes."

Cobblestone Road has given me back inspiration. The people I work with have not only been there and back, but they are still going through being alone in this world.

There is no measurement for the limit of troubles we can withstand. I relate to the tenants, to their aloneness and persistence. They've been down the same road that I have, and that road does straighten out with time and understanding. Hearing their variety of experiences has made me stronger.

Angel reminded me that a French philosopher once said: " 'What we hear we tend to forget. What we see we tend to remember. But what we do, we tend to understand.' It's more than a 'jerk' syndrome, and more than Tourette. It's dealing with acceptance. And that's what I've learned."

"There are simply those who are diagnosed, and those who aren't diagnosed," argues Ralph, who works on the computer at Cobblestone. The agency has an E-mail dialogue among members. People who are served by Community Access are now called "consumers," and the term case manager has been changed to service coordinator, because a person is not a "case." On the computer screen consumers talk to each other under the heading "crazy and proud." I am one of them in that I'm proud to have been a part of it.

Maybe it is about tolerance. All we have in this world is each other. And we are all different yet bound by our humanity. Angel's voice echoed through my mind: "It's more than a 'jerk' syndrome." I think about what has really stood out over the past few years: Evan and his fight to stay alive; my friendship with Oliver and the world of people with Tourette we met; Susanna and the love we once shared, now gone. What stands in highest relief are not the specifics of our differences but the experience of companionship where we connect.

■ ■ ■

Third Street was bright, sunny, and cold. Even this block, with its burned-out buildings and itinerant street dwellers, looked full of hope. I could see my breath, and I shouted Tourettically leaving Angel's apartment building. A lost-looking woman on the street commented on me in a trance-like communication to no one. I thought about the story Angel had just related to me, and the turmoil he has seen. Susanna had once given me a small tape recorder, which I held tightly in my left hand. I thought about my marriage. So tentative is each moment, day, and week. My thoughts drifted to Evan, now ten years past his transplant. What a strong life force he must have had to cling to life against all odds for so long.

As the woman on Third Street approached, I noticed her talking to herself. For a moment, she imitated my noises. "He barked like a dog," I heard her say. I walked straight by her.

# Afterword

Neal R. Swerdlow, M.D., Ph.D.

*Who in the rainbow can draw the line where the violet
tint ends and the orange tint begins? Distinctly we see
the difference of the colors, but where exactly
does the one first blendingly enter into the other?*
—Herman Melville, *Billy Budd*

We know much more about Tourette Syndrome (TS) than
we know about "Touretters." As Lowell Handler recognized,
each person with TS "has it differently": their thoughts, behaviors, personalities, and life experiences reflect complex
influences that cannot simply be attributed to the brain
processes that underlie the motor and vocal tics that are
the clinical criteria for a diagnosis of TS. Lowell tells of
shared experiences among Touretters, both in their symptoms and in the reactions their symptoms elicit from the
people around them. But the most compelling characteristics of each individual we meet through Lowell come not

from the tics caused by their TS, but instead from the blurry boundaries between the "syndrome" and the person.

Science is not comfortable with blurry boundaries. What we know about the biology of TS comes first from studying the distinct "colors," the places in the rainbow where violet is truly violet and orange, orange. The general strategy in research is to first solve the simplest case scenario and to then build toward the complex—like finding the framing pieces of the jigsaw puzzle before moving toward the center. Similarly TS scientists' focus has been primarily on the most observable targets and the ones that cause the most distress and dysfunction: phonic, motor, and sensory tics, and the disturbing, most common comorbid conditions such as obsessive-compulsive disorder (OCD) and attention deficit disorder (ADHD). Because of the tireless efforts spearheaded by the Tourette Syndrome Association (TSA), great energies have been directed toward understanding both the genetic and neurologic mechanisms responsible for these symptoms, and much research done to identify the best medication and nonmedication treatments. Less suited to scientific inquiry have been TS features better captured in literature rather than studied systematically: the "quick quirkiness" and "Balinese dance" as described in Dr. Goldberg's Foreword, the energies that drive the urges, the contours of sound and shape and texture that fuel Lowell's TS experience.

Science is not well suited to easily analyze the TS experience that Lowell captures in his photographs. But science advances through studies, and some studies conclude that disorders affecting dopamine, the brain chemical most implicated in the pathology of TS, alter the properties of color vision. By "translating scenes into black and white," Lowell really does recreate his Tourette's mind's eye, and when the photo editor for *Life* examines Lowell's black-and-white view of Art Bailey, we see *Life* imitating Art on multiple levels. But understanding the science of vision will not demystify the photographer's mind's eye, and learning the connection between dopamine and color vision will not explain or diminish the intensity of Lowell's photographs.

Still, science has made gigantic strides in understanding the biology of the "simplest" features of TS. In the 1960s, the Handlers ran smack into the myth that poor family dynamics cause TS. Science has since exposed this myth and replaced it with a clear appreciation that TS and its related conditions arise from abnormalities in brain function and that the family's role resides primarily in coping with, adjusting to, and taking control of the symptoms. Parents can respond with "care, direction, and love," as Lowell's did, even if at times the love must be tough and tripods broken. But science has helped us understand that TS is never *caused* by poor parenting and that the dynamics responsible for the development of TS come primarily from the complex interplay of DNA, which, after all, is the most common means of becoming a parent.

We know that TS is inherited or, more precisely, that a vulnerability to developing TS is inherited. Lowell introduced us to Jared and Joel, the identical twins with syncopated movements. Identical twins have identical DNA, and if one twin has tics, there's about a ninety percent chance that the other one will as well. In the simplest approximation, this means that TS is about ninety percent genetic. It's indeed likely that there are nongenetic triggers that can affect vulnerable individuals. Some of these may include injuries sustained in the perinatal (around birth) period, like the "difficult and dangerous labour . . . [of] a poor diseased infant" that Samuel Johnson described. Actually, because most TS identical twins aren't as "syncopated" as Jared and Joel, environmental factors do appear to modify the expression of the disorder. We also know that TS affects boys three to four times more often than girls, that it emerges in childhood, and that by age twenty about half of TS patients experience a substantial reduction in their symptoms. We've learned that TS is much more common than was once believed, perhaps occurring in as much as one percent of the population. Lowell is right: "People everywhere have Tourette; it's not as rare as we think."

One possible environmental TS trigger in vulnerable individuals has gained a lot of attention in recent years. Virtually every schoolkid in the United States (and in most developed countries) has been exposed to strep throat, an infection caused by the streptococcus bacteria. In rare cases, vulnerable children develop secondary reactions, caused by their immune system's response to the strep infection, called an autoimmune response. This autoimmune response can damage the heart or kidneys, and sometimes it can damage the basal ganglia in the brain, producing a severe reaction of abnormal movements and psychological changes. This condition is called Sydenham's chorea. Evidence, still viewed by many as controversial, suggests that a minority of cases of TS may result from a biological process similar to that which causes Sydenham's chorea—an autoimmune reaction against the basal ganglia triggered by strep throat or perhaps other infections. This phenomenon is getting a great deal of scientific and medical scrutiny, and clinical trials are currently assessing the effectiveness of a broad range of medical interventions in strep-related tic disorders, from antibiotics to immune system modulators.

Genetic studies have clarified that, unlike Huntington's disease (HD), TS is not caused by one gene but rather by several. An educated guess is that the number of TS genes is more than two and less than ten—perhaps similar in genetic complexity to more common conditions such as diabetes, hypertension, and schizophrenia. Lowell's TS symptoms are both similar to and different from his father's "constant stream of sounds . . . [and] quiet hyperactivity" likely because of the particular combinations of genes that Lowell inherited. Ironically, one challenge faced by scientists studying TS genetics that generally doesn't arise in the study of other neurologic disorders like HD is the statistical complexity created by bilineality. Bilineality happens when two individuals with TS produce children with TS (like Jeff and Cindy in chapter 9, who so aptly reason, "who better to understand them growing up than us?"). Other studies have demonstrated that TS runs more often in families who also have the comorbid conditions of OCD and ADHD. It is suspected that four different "types" of OCD often seen in TS patients may reflect the involvement of different disease genes.

## Afterword

In terms of TS neurobiology, studies have identified many components of the "wiring diagram" of the basal ganglia, which is more complicated than the wiring in your TV, a lot tougher to access, and comes with no instructions. Neuroimaging studies have revealed specific regions within the basal ganglia—like the caudate nucleus—where both the size and chemical composition differ between TS and non-TS individuals. By studying the way chemicals work in these brain regions, science is leading us toward "smarter" medications for TS—ones that avoid some of the side effects that Lowell described but maximize the benefits he also experienced. For example, one receptor in these brain regions binds chemicals called cannabinoids, which are contained in the marijuana Lowell found initially helpful, but proved so devastating to his relationships, and ultimately nearly cost him his life. Now scientists are studying ways to use these or related chemicals in safer, medication forms that ideally will suppress tics without bringing the kind of havoc marijuana did to Lowell.

While many new treatments for individuals with TS are on the horizon, medical science has already identified a number that are safe, effective, and available right now. Certainly the most important one is the vastly improved knowledge about TS in the medical community. One poignant theme throughout Lowell's chapters is that ignorance and stigmatization are among the most devastating things for those with TS. In the past, people didn't know what TS was and what it wasn't. Perhaps the greatest of the TSA's many triumphs has been its widespread success in educating physicians, families, teachers, and the general public about TS. When Lowell was growing up, it was a rare physician or schoolteacher who recognized TS for what it was. Today, public schools across the United States benefit from professional in-services sponsored by the TSA. Every U.S.-trained medical student is taught about TS. Textbooks, journal articles, educational videotapes, magazines, talk shows, movies, sitcoms, and countless Websites contain information on TS. If you want to know about TS, you need not rely on translations of the nineteenth-century works of Gilles de la Tourette; just search Google. The TSA's massive public relations effort has led to earlier detection and prompt and more appropriate treatments for literally millions of people. Educating patients, families, teachers, and health care professionals about TS is hands down the safest and most effective first treatment option.

Based on the outcomes of careful clinical trials, physicians now have available numerous medications for many symptoms experienced by individuals with TS. The key issue is to know exactly which symptoms to treat. Studies have shown that functional impairment in TS is most often caused by the comorbid symptoms, as described throughout Lowell's tale: obsessions, compulsions, attention deficits, and sometimes rage attacks. It is less common that, in the absence of these symptoms, motor or vocal tics alone will cause significant functional impairment. More often, tics are a source of discomfort for bystanders. As Lowell noted, "people who were especially nervous or uncomfortable with themselves were most bothered. . . . People in close proximity . . . thought I was mocking them." This is an important guide in treatment, because there are many safe, effective medications for obsessions, compulsions, attention deficits, and rage attacks, while medications that suppress tics per se can be challenging due to side effects such as sedation, weight gain, and others. Interestingly, studies show that, in many people, medications that effectively target the comorbid symptoms—even stimulants used to treat ADHD—can also reduce tic severity.

Some disorders of the frontal lobes and basal ganglia may be responsive not only to medications, but also to non-medication therapies, including specific forms of behavioral therapy. Lowell's "diligent practice" led to dramatic improvement in his speech because, with diligence and practice, the brain (and particularly the caudate nucleus) can change itself. Yes, Bate was right: "the mind has a mind of its own," but in its ability to regulate the brain, it finds a way to not be so "unpredictable and erratic." In effect, the answer to Lowell's question about free will in TS is that it is not completely lost, but it does take diligent practice to exercise it. Studies of brain metabolism in persons with OCD have shown that cognitive and behavioral therapies not only reduce symptoms, but also correct the abnormalities in the frontal lobes and caudate nucleus. This doesn't mean that tics will just go away if you "try harder." That would be like saying that you can play Mozart without piano lessons if you just "try harder." Maybe some can, but for most people, it would take a long time and be very frustrating. To be effective, behavioral therapy must be learned and practiced correctly. The type of behavioral therapy that appears to be most helpful in TS is called habit reversal therapy (HRT). Studies supported by the TSA are now examining the efficacy of HRT at several large clinical centers in the United States, while smaller studies are examining brain changes that might occur over the course of symptom improvement with HRT treatment.

Diligence has also sustained free will at the level of the TS community and its connection with society. When

# Afterword

Lowell Handler stepped to the microphone at the Food and Drug Administration to advocate for the needs of people with TS, he demonstrated his free will in a powerful way. When families formed the TSA more than thirty years ago, they brought this diligence to a national and now an international level. By uniting families with TS and offering them an opportunity to advocate for themselves as a group, the TSA has focused enormous energies toward scientific discovery and medical advances for TS. Individuals and families are active in many ways, especially through their support of and participation in TS outreach and research. This diligence builds on itself: strong family and organizational commitment attracts medical scientists to focus on problems relevant to TS, and the TSA has been highly successful in engaging the resources and efforts of the National Institutes of Health in studies seeking to uncover the causes of and improving treatments for TS. As the TSA has brought together couples like Lowell's friends David and Hannah, and many thousands of families throughout the United States and abroad, the collective "Tourette response" has been to use the powerful tool of their free will to shape their future and that of their children.

What will be the future gains in TS science and medicine? What will be the "better things" to come in Lowell's epigraph? Obviously, nobody knows for certain, but some general, long-term predictions can be made. First, clinical trials will continue to develop safer, more effective treatments and will identify more accurately those who benefit from different types of treatments. Second, a number of genes that convey a vulnerability to developing TS will be identified. Using information gained about the normal physiology of the basal ganglia, studies will determine what these TS genes do and, more importantly, what they do wrong in individuals with TS. Treatments will be developed that specifically target the consequences of these abnormal gene processes, thereby blunting the expression of TS symptoms or perhaps even preventing the development of symptoms in children who carry particular TS genes. Third, science will identify the link between autoimmune processes and less common but more treatment-resistant forms of TS, and science will develop ways to protect vulnerable individuals from their own immune system's onslaught. Fourth, as the genetic and neurobiological underpinnings of TS become clearer, societal awareness of TS will increase, and stigmatization will continue to decline.

But nowhere in the future of TS science and medicine do I see anything that should worry Paige, the flutist and conductor. TS families joining together to enhance our understanding of TS and find ways to reduce suffering in no way threatens the uniqueness, the open-mindedness, or the quick quirkiness of some individuals who have TS. People will always have eccentricities and idiosyncrasies— people will always be more dynamic and interesting than their TS symptoms. But as Lowell's tales tell us, there are times when the symptoms of TS can shackle the spirit, can pummel it with energies that range from distracting and unproductive to devastating and dehumanizing. And have no fear, relieving suffering by diminishing these symptoms won't diminish the depth of life's experience for people with TS. Surely, there's no shortage of suffering in life: leukemia, marital discord, AIDS, depression, drug addiction, and existential angst are parts of Lowell's stories that won't go away once we cure TS. TS science and medicine have been, and should continue to be, guided by the TS families who support it, using the TSA as the vehicle to maintain this oversight. TS families will direct science and medicine toward preventing the suffering caused by the darker sides of TS and, at the same time, will understand and respect the uniqueness of Touretters. The future of TS science and medicine is in the hands of families with TS. Among all of earth's cultures, are there any more qualified to protect their hope for better things to come?

# RESOURCES .

# FACTS ABOUT TOURETTE SYNDROME

## ANSWERS TO THE MOST COMMONLY ASKED QUESTIONS

*What is Tourette Syndrome?*
It is a neurobiological disorder characterized by tics—involuntary, rapid, sudden movements and/or vocal outbursts that occur repeatedly.

*What are the most common symptoms?*
Symptoms change periodically in number, frequency, type and severity—even disappearing for weeks or months at a time. Commonly, motor tics may be eye blinking, head jerking, shoulder shrugging, facial grimacing. Vocally—throat clearing, barking noises, sniffing and tongue clicking.

*Where does the name come from?*
The first case was reported in 1825 by a French neurologist, Dr. Georges Gilles de la Tourette, for whom the disorder was named.

## What is the cause of the syndrome?

No definite cause has yet been established, but considerable evidence points to abnormal metabolism of at least one brain chemical called dopamine.

## How many people are affected?

As Tourette Syndrome often goes undiagnosed, no exact figure can be given. But authoritative estimates indicate that some 200,000 in the United States are known to have the disorder. All races and ethnic groups are affected.

## Is it inherited?

Genetic studies indicate that TS is inherited as a dominant gene, with about 50% chance of passing the gene from parent to child. Sons are three to four times more likely than daughters to exhibit Tourette Syndrome symptoms.

## Is obscene language (coprolalia) a typical symptom of TS?

Definitely not. The fact is that cursing, uttering obscenities, and ethnic slurs are manifested by fewer than 15 percent of people with TS. Too often, however, the media seize upon this symptom for its sensational effect.

## Do outbursts of personal, ethnic and other slurs by people with TS reflect their true feelings?

On the contrary. The very rare use of ethnic slurs stems from an uncontrollable urge to voice the forbidden even when it is *directly opposite* to the actual beliefs of the person voicing it.

## How is TS diagnosed?

Diagnosis is made by observing symptoms and evaluating the history of their onset. No blood analysis, X-ray or other type of medical test can identify this condition. The TS symptoms usually emerge between 5 and 18 years of age.

## *How is it treated?*

While there is no cure, medication is available to help control the symptoms. Among the drugs currently in use are haloperidol (Haldol), clonidine (Catapres) and pimozide (Orap).

## *Is there ever a remission?*

Many people with TS get better, not worse, as they mature. In a small minority of cases symptoms remit completely in adulthood.

## *Do TS children have special educational needs?*

As a group, children with TS have the same IQ range as the population at large. But problems in dealing with tics, often combined with attention deficits and other learning difficulties, may call for special education assistance. Examples of teaching strategies include: technical help such as tape recorders, typewriters or computers to assist reading and writing and access to tutoring in a resource room. Under federal law, an identification as "handicapped" or "other health impaired" entitles the student to an Individual Education Plan.

## *What future faces TS people?*

In general people with TS lead productive lives and can anticipate a normal life span. Despite problems of varying severity, many reach high levels of achievement and number in their ranks as surgeons, psychiatrists, teachers and professional athletes.

## *What is the Tourette Syndrome Association?*

TSA is the only national voluntary health organization dedicated to identifying the cause, finding the cure and controlling the effects of this disorder. Its programs of research, professional and public education and individual and family services are made possible through the generosity of donors.

Reprinted by permission of the Tourette Syndrome Association.

*Resources*

# ORGANIZATIONS

For more information about Tourette syndrome, you can contact the following organizations:

Tourette Syndrome Association
42-40 Bell Boulevard, Suite 205
Bayside, NY 11361-2820
Telephone: (718) 224-2999
Fax: (718) 279-9596
www.tsa-usa.org

Obsessive-Compulsive Foundation, Inc.
676 State Street
New Haven, CT 06511
Telephone: (203) 401-2070
Fax: (203) 401-2076
www.ocfoundation.org

Children and Adults with Attention-Deficit/Hyperactivity Disorder (CHADD)
8181 Professional Place, Suite 150
Landover, MD 20785
Telephone: (301) 306-7070
Fax: (301) 306-7090
www.chadd.org
National Resource Center on AD/HD (800) 233-4050

National Organization for Rare Disorders (NORD)
55 Kenosia Avenue
P.O. Box 1968
Danbury, CT 06813-1968
Telephone: (203) 744-0100
Toll-free: (800) 999-6673 (voicemail only)
TDD Number: (203) 797-9590
Fax: (203) 798-2291
www.rarediseases.org

*Twitch and Shout* is an award-winning hour-long film that provides an intimate journey into the startling world of Tourette syndrome. Through the eyes of Lowell Handler, the film introduces the viewer to other individuals with Tourette syndrome, including an artist, an actress, a professional basketball player, and a Mennonite lumberjack. *Twitch and Shout* is an emotionally absorbing, sometimes unsettling, and ultimately uplifting film about people who must contend with a society that often sees them as crazy or bad—and a body and mind that won't do what they are told. "What a wonderful, compassionate, funny, instructive, inspiring, and flat-out brilliant documentary. *Twitch and Shout* is likely to change your opinions, or change you, period. It doesn't get much better than this." *(New York Daily News)*

For rental or purchase information about *Twitch and Shout* contact:

New Day Films
190 Route 17M
P.O. Box 1084
Harriman, NY 10926

Telephone: (888) 367-9154
Fax: (845) 774-2945
www.newday.com

# ACKNOWLEDGMENTS

The first and foremost thanks must go to my two editors, Deirdre Mullane at Dutton, and Adair Rowland, my friend of twenty years and personal confidante. The entire project would not have reached fruition without Andrew Blauner, my literary agent, whose foresight, along with Deirdre's and Adair's, helped me realize this book.

There have been many people who have helped me, including everyone at Blue Mountain Center, where I wrote part of the manuscript; Laurel Chiten, producer, director, and writer of the film *Twitch and Shout*, who coined the title; Jenny Cox for help with the final outline; Elkhonon Goldberg for his insights; Michael Gold for first publishing my writing in *In Health*; Fran Gordon for being herself; Enid Handler for insightfully helping with early chapters;

# Acknowledgments

Lisa Kogan at *Elle* for editing "Jet Set Tourette"; Kraine Gallery Bar (KGB) for being a great place to read and drink; all the folks at Naked Angels for letting me give readings of some of the chapters as I worked on them; Oliver Sacks for whatever he does; Michael Robinson for help with the quote from the Bible; Jeff Wheelwright, who first developed the story on Tourette's syndrome for *Life* magazine; Ann and David Yeadon for much help with the early outline; and last but important, all those who are profiled and interviewed in this book.

**Lowell Handler** is a photojournalist whose work has appeared in many publications, including *Life, Newsweek, U.S. News & World Report, Elle,* the *Sunday Times Magazine* (London), the *New York Times,* and the *Boston Globe.* His photographs have been exhibited in the United States and Europe, and he was associate producer and narrator for the Emmy-nominated PBS documentary *Twitch and Shout.* He lives with his wife, writer Jane Smith, in Rhinecliff, New York, and teaches photography at Dutchess Community College.

**Elkhonon Goldberg** is a clinical professor of neurology at New York University Medical Center and director of the Institute of Neuropsychology and Cognitive Performance.

**Neal R. Swerdlow, M.D.,** is professor of psychiatry at the University of California, San Diego, and chair of the Scientific Advisory Board of the Tourette Syndrome Association.